GET YOUR HEART ON

SUPER LOVE
SHOUT OUTS FOR
Gia + Get Your
Heart On

"If you have been sitting back, longing to contribute more to the world but not knowing how, *Get Your Heart On* is what you've been looking for! Gia's fun and accessible book will inspire you to find the perfect way for your gifts to make a difference in the world."

— **PAMELA SLIM**, award-winning author of *Body of Work*, speaker and business consultant

"If you are struggling or at a stalling point in your journey of charity work, *Get Your Heart On* is a great book to get you going again. It will get you charged and ready to be the positive change that is needed in the world."

— **BRANDON BLACKBERN**, firefighter and all-around do-gooder

"Gia's generous book is the perfect blend of full-on inspiration and actionable, tangible tips guaranteed to help any change maker create their positive impact in the world in a doable, and yes, epic, way."

— **DEBBIE REBER**, New York Times bestselling author and founder of TiLT Parenting

"Gia has a passion for people and causes and a superpower for igniting fires in bellies!"

— **JOY BURKHARD,** founder and executive director at 2020 Mom

"*Get Your Heart On* inspired me and gave me hope. Gia's infectious love, support, and wisdom will help you figure out who you are and why, along with how to create your highest purpose for your life." — **JULIA PICETTI,** speaker and substance recovery advocate

"I wish I had met Gia earlier in my life and career—her kind of enthusiasm will pull the whole room forward with her! Filled with wisdom and love for all, *Get Your Heart On* gives the even grumpiest of us the permission to have fun growing and learning. She offers countless brilliant snippets of wisdom, simple exercises, and a zest for life that is contagious. Pick a page, any page. Welcome to Gia's world!"

— **BRET STEPHENSON, MA,** author of *From Boys to Men: Spiritual Rites of Passage in an Indulgent Age* and *The Undercurrents of Adolescence: Tracking the Evolution of Modern Adolescence and Delinquency Through Classic Cinema*

"As a middle school teacher, I seek inspiration on a daily basis to help me create a learning environment with creativity, compassion, and connection, and *Get Your Heart On* gave me the tools, confidence, and determination to lead my students with optimism. In reading this book, I felt as if Gia was alongside me throughout the whole journey! If you want to truly make a difference, *Get Your Heart On* will be the motivational guide to ensure that your purpose leaves a lasting impression." — **MARK KEIM,** middle school teacher

"Gia Duke is one of those incredible humans whose heart is approximately the size of the BLUE WHALE (roughly VW Bug sized...v. big). I highly recommend spending time in her magical sphere!"

— **SARAH SEIDELMANN, MD,** author *Swimming with Elephants*, life coach, and shamanic healer

"*Get Your Heart On* is an authentic roadmap for helping people take their happiness to new heights. Gia's unique ability to understand, relate to, and inspire people from all walks of life makes this a book that will keep readers smiling all the way through."

— **JAMES "JAMEY" BREEN,** speaker and author of *Keep it Rollin*

"If an avalanche (movement/action) begins with a single snowflake (person/idea) than Gia would be that snowflake. Her new book *Get Your Heart On* provides the KEY to triggering the avalanche. A must read for those who want to make a difference!"

— **SKIP DUKE,** retired high school teacher, coach and guidance counselor (not to mention Gia's dad)

"Gia is a gem! As a person who spends every waking hour working to motivate others to take action on climate change, I have always said that it will be the love revolution that saves us all. This book not only provides the spark for a love revolution, but also the key ingredients for making it happen. Read it and join the revolution—we need everyone everywhere doing everything all the time as quickly as possible!"

— **JILL MACINTYRE WITT,** professor, speaker, activist, and author of the *Climate Justice Field Manual*

GET YOUR HEART ON

The How-To Guide for People Who Want to Make a Difference

WHERE TO START. WHAT TO DO.
AND HOW TO KICK ASS ALONG THE WAY.

gia Duke

GET YOUR HEART ON

Subtitle: The How-To Guide for People Who Want to Make a Difference. Where to start. What to do. And how to kick ass along the way.
By Gia Duke

An Imprint of Timber Sky Publishing
Get Your Heart On is a registered
trademark of Gia Duke Productions LLC
ISBN: 978-0-9998125-0-1
Edited by Deborah Reber
Cover + Layout Design by The Book Designers
Sketch Art by David Cohen aka Doodleslice
About Author Photograph by Kelly Nicolaisen

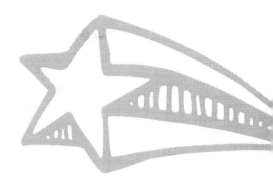

DEDICATION

For my three boys // Justin + Tobin + Blaze (our pup)

You rock my **LOVE** world every single day. Thank you for being by my side. So grateful to share life's adventure with you.

For Shasta and Timber, my two rescue doggies and heart reasons that kept me going for so many years. Even if only one reader becomes inspired to help shelter animals like you, it would all be worth it (and they'd forever be as lucky as I am). You're *always* with me.

This book is also dedicated to anyone who believes that one person can make a difference. We need you and your big heart now more than ever.

FREE WORKBOOK

As a special thank you for showing up each day as your awesome self and being a part of my Super Love Revolution, I created a free sidekick, **THE GET YOUR HEART ON WORKBOOK.** with all of the exercises from this book, just for you!

TO GRAB YOUR FREE GET YOUR HEART ON WORKBOOK.

go to www.giaduke.com/getyourhearton

SAY HELLO // LET'S CONNECT

Come on over to the online hotspot for our big-hearted community to say hello and get in on the conversation!

Website: **GiADUKE.COM**

Email me at: hello@giaduke.com. I love hearing from you!

YOU CAN ALSO FIND ME HERE:

FB // facebook.com/Gia-Duke

Instagram // giaduke

Hashtag // #getyourhearton

Pinterest // giaduke

THE HEARTLINE

Call anytime for a little spontaneous inspiration, love, or feel good message from me to you. (Inspired by one of my all time fav authors SARK)

THE HEARTLINE: 415-436-JRAD (723) - 24 HOURS A DAY

Check it out. Give it a call. Share with your friends. It's Super Duper Fun!

FYI: It rings about 5xs before the message begins -

Retro Style: like old school phones :)

TOC//

GET YOUR HEART ON

The How-To Guide for People
Who Want to Make a Difference

WHERE TO START. WHAT TO DO.
AND HOW TO KICK ASS ALONG THE WAY.

iNTRODUCTiON

RAD. You're here! That can only mean one thing—you're ready to get your givin' on! That's right. The word on the street is that you're here to make a difference in the world.

The only problem is…

Maybe you're ready to go but you're not sure where you're headed. In fact, you may have no idea where or how to start. Or maybe you're afraid to begin because you might mess up or make the wrong choice and you're frustrated because you know the only one holding you back is you.

You spend time watching other people doing super cool give-back work and wonder why you just can't get your own shizz together. Or you feel like time is just passing by and you're not taking any action. If only someone or something could give you direction or guidance along the way…

Been there. I understand. And I'm here to help.

But before you dive in, here's a quick ditty about the pages you're holding in your hand (or lookin' at on your screen).

HOW TO USE THIS BOOK

This book is yours.
Use it however you want to. Pick it up whenever you need it.

Dig in. Jump out. Flip around.

LET IT SUPPORT YOU. GUIDE YOU. INSPIRE YOU.
LET IT HELP YOU GET WHAT YOU CAME FOR.

Get out those Sharpies. Write in it. Draw in it.
Put stickers on pages and highlight your favorite sections.
Cross things off or out. Make it work for you.

That's right, recess is in session!
And there won't be any whistles blowin' on this playground.

It's time. So head on over to your favorite cozy spot, grab a yummy drink, light a candle or set off some fireworks, and begin. Feel free to devour the whole shebang in one sitting or just skip around as you please. But whatever you do, don't be fooled by its size, cuz there's *whole lotta juice* in here. **And the super bonus (more like cherry on top), because that's how we do things around here?**

You'll walk away knowing you're not doing it all alone. In fact, you'll be connected to an amazing group of big-hearted people who are ready to do more, care more, and support one another.

Did I mention this is so much more than just a book? That's right, my friend. I've created a special online community to connect us in real time. And believe me when I say there are some pretty badass people you're gonna wanna meet, and who are waiting to meet you.

i BELiEVE

I BELIEVE...
We're not meant to be alone.

I believe...
Empathy matters.

I believe...
Heart is Hot. Kindness is sexy.

I believe...
What you feel in your heart counts.

I KNOW...
The only thing that can hold you back or move you forward is yourself.

I know...
Being kind lives after we die.

I know...
There's no such thing as too much love in the world.

I know...
We are all connected.
It's not just about me. It's about we.

I know...
One person does make a difference.

A TOAST!

If you were standing in front of me…

I'd give you a big hug, 'cuz I'm a super hugger. And even if you pulled away a little, or let your arms hang stiff by your sides, I'd still wrap my arms around you for a quick squeeze. And then I'd ask you what drives you, what inspires you, and what makes you feel alive. Most importantly, I'd ask you what kind of difference you want to make in the world and how I can help.

I promise that if you just do *one* thing after reading this book to spread some love, to help someone, to care a little bit more than you already do, your heart will smile brighter and the world will be grateful.

Oh, and there's one more thing you have to know before you read on.

THIS IS SO MUCH MORE THAN A BOOK.
THIS IS A BEGINNING.

In fact, it's the start of something bigger than I can even imagine right now.
How do I know?

I can **FEEL** it.
And after you read this, I hope you can feel it too.

Now, to kick this off right . . . **A TOAST!**

Raise your glass.
Hold it up high.

CHEERS TO YOU AND ALL THE INCREDIBLE PEOPLE WE HAVE YET TO MEET WHO ARE READY TO DO SOME SERIOUS GOOD TOGETHER.

—Here! Here!

Clink! Clink! Clink!
LET'S GET THIS PARTY STARTED!

Do me one favor, though—don't just read this book. **LIVE IT.**

You Ready?
Open it up! Dig in!
Read on!

(I'm so happy you're here.)

Big Hugs + Love,
xox, *gia*

HER EYES. THAT'S WHERE HOPE LIES

There's a reason I have the word *Matter* tattooed on the top of my right wrist facing me. "Backwards" as the tattoo artist told me. I had it placed there years ago so I could see it everyday.

I chose this word carefully. But even so, I'd hear things like, "What's that say? Matter? You mean, like *gray matter*?" Or they'd snicker. "Matter? Like, it just doesn't matter?" Another giggle.

Nope and nope.

I chose the word *matter* because it's what I strive for. I'm here to make a difference in the world and to help others do the same. I want my life to matter and I want the people I cross paths with to know that their lives matter, too.

But before I go any further, I'm gonna push the rewind button.

Do you remember that segment on *Sesame Street* that featured a big square on the screen divided into four smaller squares and a song that went, "One of these kids is doing their own thing…now it's time to play our game"?

And then in three of the smaller squares there would be a kid doing something similar: dribbling a basketball, shooting baskets, spinning the basketball on their finger. In the fourth square a kid would be doing something totally different—cartwheels or skateboard tricks or dancing. Kids in the viewing audience at home were asked to guess which kid is doing their own thing.

WELL THAT KiD iN BOX FOUR? THAT'S ME.

I'm the girl who loves to create, perform, and try new things. I love the energy of being around lots of different kinds of people. I crave change and have to do things in my own way.

I love connecting with people, sharing stories, and laughing so hard that no sound comes out of my mouth. I love to play charades, dance in the rain, hang in funky coffee shops, and host hugathons. I secretly wish I could star on Broadway and ride cross country on a motorcycle.

I dream big dreams and have chased many of them.

Looking back, I've realized how much of my being able to explore who I was and what I loved as a kid was due to my parents' support. Although I'm sure there were and still are many times where they shook their heads and looked at each other wondering what their crazy daughter was up to next, they never told me I couldn't do something or try something new. I believed anything was possible.

I also learned at an early age that life is short, definitely not always fair, and that not everybody grew up or lived like I did. I noticed when someone was having a hard time at school or if they looked sad or were left out or getting picked on...especially if they were alone.

That wasn't okay with me.

I've had enough WTF moments to light a fire under my booty and remind me to go after what I want. I've also learned how to figure out what really matters most during my mom's long, slow memory loss journey. I know that now is the time to do and be who I want to be. I'm so not gonna wait for someday. And I don't want you to either.

You see, *compassion, empathy,* and *love* have always been my driver.

HEART FIRST. THAT'S HOW i ROLL.

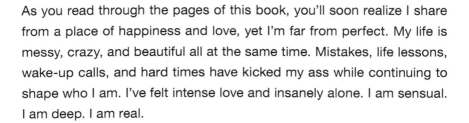

As you read through the pages of this book, you'll soon realize I share from a place of happiness and love, yet I'm far from perfect. My life is messy, crazy, and beautiful all at the same time. Mistakes, life lessons, wake-up calls, and hard times have kicked my ass while continuing to shape who I am. I've felt intense love and insanely alone. I am sensual. I am deep. I am real.

There have been many times when I've wanted to walk away from my difference-making dreams and just quit because it hurts too much. I own and honor my experiences and work on letting go of the things I can't control.

I've spent many sleepless nights (let's be honest . . . *years*) thinking about all of the pain in the world. I'd imagine all the people or animals who were sick, struggling, or hanging on with hope or grasping for just one small break. I would close my eyes and instead of quietly dreaming, I'd hear their voices or see their faces in my mind telling me to not give up or walk away. Then the tears would start to roll down my cheeks because I had no idea what to do or how to begin. **And that not knowing piece? Damn that was hard.**

Eventually, some time would pass and I'd snap out of my funk long enough to remind myself that I can figure this out. Somehow. Some way. **And for a moment, I'd believe it.** Long enough anyway, to keep moving forward, even though I had no idea where I was going.

I was the girl who ached for purpose and so badly wanted to find people who felt like I did. I wanted to find my tribe. But the people I related to most at the time had no idea who I was or they were dead.

I call them my imaginary friends. And they keep me going.

I'm talking the big world changers, activists, love leaders, peacemakers, creators, artists, musicians, and poets.

I'd imagine what kind of advice Martin Luther King Jr., Oprah, or Mahatma Gandhi would give me over a cup of coffee. I'd picture the stories I would hear from Nelson Mandela, Paul Watson (Sea Shepherd), or Ingrid Newkirk (founder of PETA) while we were out on a walk together.

I would tear their pictures out of magazines and post them up on my office wall. I'd dance to their music, read their books, and let their powerful words and visions guide me.

My imaginary friends are real-life examples of people who inspire me and show me what is possible. And whenever I'd hit a bump along the way, I would look at my big wall of faces.

I'd remind myself that If they could do something as huge as fighting for civil rights, speaking up against animal cruelty, taking a stand for peace, or literally risking their life by putting their small boat between a ship's harpoon and a defenseless whale, I can keep going. I must.

Then, with my newfound inspiration, I'd keep going, and take one more step toward my heart.

I spent a large portion of my life runnin' around from cause to cause doing whatever I could to help. To advocate. Raise funds. Spread the word, cheer on, or hold hands. **I became the rescue girl. But there were too many causes that needed support and only one me.** I felt like I couldn't help fast enough and no matter what I did there was always so much more work to be done.

I wouldn't change a thing about my journey, but as you might have guessed, **over time I started to feel run down and exhausted.** I was a lone wolf on a love mission with no light at the end of the tunnel.

I had to pace myself. And so that's what I did.

I decided that the best way I could make a difference was to focus my energy on the give-back work I was most passionate about. For me that meant advocating for foster youth, helping rescue animals, and raising money and contributing my time to support causes that spoke to me.

Eventually, I began to help other people do the same thing in their own lives. People who also wanted to make a difference in their own way, but skip the part about burnout and struggle.

People like you.

That's why I wrote this book. Because I finally figured it out. It's possible to do things in a different way. A way that not only feels better, freer, and more fulfilling, but can make an even bigger impact on the world.

AT THE HEART OF iT ALL? YOU AND ME.

That's right.
We do it together.

Cuz, when it comes to giving back and making a difference, I'm your girl.

Seriously. This. Is. My. Thing.
And I'm guessing it might be your thing, too.

So, what do you say.
Are you in?

Awesome.

All together now…

HERE WE GO!

THE REVOLUTION STARTS HERE

When I was a little girl, I wanted to fly on the trapeze and join the circus. The kind where the clowns aren't creepy and the animals roam free.

I've always loved the circus vibe.

LADIES + GENTLEMEN...echo...echo...echo...

Welcome to...
THE GREATEST SHOW ON EARTH!

Drum roll, center stage, spotlight up...

Where different types of people from all walks of life come together under The Big Top to perform.

The Daring. The Brave. The Charismatic.
The Misfits. The Outcasts. The Show Stoppers.

The Music. The Colors. The Energy.
The Talent. The Passion. The Show.

A family of sorts.

Over the years, I've been creating my own kind of community where...

the passion-fueled and the kind,

the gutsy and the purpose-driven,
the leaders, creatives, underdogs, and the world igniters

…come together under the Big Top I call **Revolution Super Love**.

Our Fire. Our Drive.

Our causes may be different. But there's one thing that ties us all together—we are all here to make a difference in the world.

REVOLUTiON SUPER LOVE

It's time for a Shake-up. An Uprising. A Revolution.
Where love is riding shotgun and you're behind the wheel.

Where we take that one powerful word—L-O-V-E—and pump up the volume by working together.

We magnify it. Jumbo-size it. Ignite it.

We SUPER LOVE IT.

Revolution Super Love is like a wave of goodness and intentional kindness spreading from one caring person and on to the next. And then another one raises their hand and says, "Heck to the YEAH! I'm so in! I want to be a part of this!"

You guessed it, my friend.
You're invited.

DARE WiTH ME

In order for this Revolution to happen we've got to believe in two things:

The power of One.
The impact of Many.

And when we all choose to...care more and do more, we create a new kind of possibility, jam-packed with love.

I may have started this, but this isn't a solo crusade.

It's a Movement.
A Revolution.

AND i NEED YOU.

To get Fired Up!
To get Started!
To Go For It!

I invite you **to take action.**
Strike that.

i DARE YOU

To join Me.
To join Us.

TO COME TOGETHER TO MAKE A DIFFERENCE

What do you say?

You ready?

P.S. HEART iS H-O-T

Just in case you're not quite sure if you want to commit to diving in just yet, I'm gonna let you in on a little secret that I think is gonna make you wanna seal the deal.

Here it goes.

How would you like to make yourself sexier? Like, starting today? HELLS YEAH!

And what if I promise that you won't need to follow a fancy diet plan, drink some nutty shake concoction, or commit to the latest cleanse to make it happen. Interested? (*Is that even a question, Gia? SIGN ME UP!*)

And would you believe me if I told you that you already have every-thing you need to be hotter right now? (*Okay, now you're just talkin' crazy.*) I know, I hear ya. We've been taught to believe that if something sounds too good to be true then it probably is.

But here's the scoop. You ready for it?

HEART is H-O-T!

You know what they say about people who make a difference...
...they're sexier. That's a fact.

Here—let me show you.

Let's start with a guy. Say...

Russell Wilson, quarterback for the Seattle Seahawks. He checks a few hotness boxes from the get go. Professional athlete, check! Super Bowl Champion, check! But then our hearts *really* flutter when we find out he schedules regular visits to the Seattle Children's Hospital to share some smiles with young patients and their families. SO HOT! When we learn that he also started the *Why Not You Foundation* to help today's youth to become tomorrow's leaders? Forget about it. SMOKIN' HOT!

And then there's...

Angelina Jolie, a human rights activist on behalf of refugees. Crank up the SEXY SCALE! Ellen DeGeneres' contribution to social equality, HOT. Giving a voice to gay rights. SO HOT. Encouraging kindness to every-one, every day. HECKA HOT!

As if it's not sizzling enough to be a multi Grammy Award-winning singer, songwriter, and producer, Alicia Keys smolders with hotness with her work as a global activist in the fight against HIV/AIDS for more than a decade. Talk about meaningful impact...this is OFF THE CHARTS HOT!

This list wouldn't be complete without one of my way back hottie crushes Mr. Matt Damon. Did you know that he's so much more than Jason Bourne and Will Hunting? That's right, he's also the cofounder of a nonprofit called Water.org that is helping bring safe water and sanitation to people all over the world. HELLO HOTTIE TOTTIE!

AND DO YOU KNOW WHAT MAKES THEM ALL SO DOGGONE FLY?

(Hint: It's not their celebrity status.)
It's who they are off the screen or stage.

THEIR CHARACTER.
THEIR KINDNESS. THEIR COMPASSION.

So don't go thinking you have to be well known for your hotness factor to go up a notch. Here, I'll show you real quick. Let's take a look at the people we cross paths with every day that we can see anywhere, anytime.

Like…

The guy you didn't really notice on the bus until he got up and offered his seat to the mom-to-be who just walked on. WICKED HOT!

The girl you've had your eye on from the office who spends her Saturday afternoons playing the piano at the senior living community center where her grandpa lives. Can you say, HOT-NESS CITY?!

FACT.
HEART IS
HOT.

AND YOU KNOW WHAT?
KiNDNESS NOT ONLY LOOKS GOOD.
BUT iT FEELS GOOD. TOO.

VA-VA-VOOM!
WHAT'S NOT TO LOVE?

SERIOUSLY...
WHAT ARE YOU WAITING FOR?

LET'S BEGIN.

PART
01

DIFFERENCE MAKING 101

**I ALWAYS WONDERED WHY SOMEBODY
DIDN'T DO SOMETHING ABOUT THAT
AND THEN I REALIZED I AM SOMEBODY**

—LILY TOMLIN

Just so we all start off on the same page…

Difference Making = Doing something to help someone or something for the better.

I call it Heart-work.

HEART-WORK

Heart-work is what the Revolution Super Love lifestyle is all about.

HEART-WORK = COMPASSION IN ACTION

It's about…
Helping.
Caring. Connecting.

It's about…
Creating Hope.

Giving Back. Sharing Love.

And it's about…
Leading. Listening.
And being brave enough to start a conversation that matters.

It's about leaving a legacy and making a difference in our own way.

With heart-work, there is no finish line.
It's about what we do and who we are along the way.

THE NEW 80/20 RULE

Here it is.
Your #1 Mantra.

The only rule you really need to follow while going after your make-a-difference dreams.

Use it anytime you need to check in with yourself about a decision you're struggling with or if you want reassurance you're on the right track or you could use an extra boost to keep you moving forward.

The New 80/20 is my M.O. and I have story upon story I could share to illustrate how it has positively impacted my life and gotten me to where I want to go. From finding two of my rescue dogs, to meeting my husband, to starting a nonprofit. It's not rocket science, but sticking to it will work every time. So here it is...

The New 80/20. Redefined.

80% Heart = The reason you care
20% Guts = The courage to act

Let's dig deeper...

80% HEART

Do you know what inspires you, drives you, moves you from within, and can guide you in the right direction? THUMP. THUMP. THUMP. That's right. It's that fist-sized muscle beating to your own beautiful rhythm in your chest—your heart.

It's what makes you so stinkin' excited, moved, or pissed off enough to do something to make a difference, to trigger action.

The most important piece of anything we do is connected to our heart. Our heart is where our passion lives. It's why we care.

All we need to do is pay attention.

Tap into it.
Let it be our guide.

If you do that 80% of the time, I promise you that getting where you want to go will come naturally.

20% GUTS

One of the top reasons people don't reach their goals or even get started is fear. It takes guts to makes things happen. But how do we get it? Where do we find it? We're gonna talk about this in more detail later in the book but for now, here's the nitty gritty.

Ever see the heart-warming movie, *We Bought a Zoo*? One of my favorite parts is when the recently widowed father Benjamin Mee offers his teenage son this invaluable advice: "You know, sometimes all you need is twenty seconds of insane courage. Just literally twenty seconds of just embarrassing bravery. And I promise you, something great will come of it." So true, right?

Because twenty seconds is about all it takes for us to kick something into action. In fact, sometimes for me twenty seconds is actually too long. I say it takes about six seconds of courage.

Six seconds to…

Walk through the door.
Start a conversation. Say hello.
Push Publish. Hit Send.
Turn on the microphone.
Begin.

If you need a few other secret weapons like that Wonder Woman bra you're rockin' under your shirt or that Superman belt buckle you're wearing, we won't tell. Or if you want to channel some of your imaginary friends like I do, then by all means, do that.

Going after what you want can be intimidating at times. **To make your goals happen, you've gotta be willing to do what the other guy won't.** You've gotta have the guts.

Play along with me...

Can you think of a time when you took a chance on something and you had no idea what the outcome would be? Or when you had the mojo to do something or say something you were maybe a little afraid of?

What inspired your courage to act? What made you feel fearless, even if only for six seconds? What were your bold moments?

And how did you feel afterwards? Awe-Yeah!
Who knew you had it in you?

If you're still on the fence about stepping into something that's important to you, ask yourself this one question:

Will I regret not doing it?

There's your answer.

i PLAY THE GUiTAR ⚡

My guy Justin and our teenage son Tobin recently went to a Green Day concert. Halfway through the show, they saw a boy about Tobin's age toward the front of the crowd holding up a sign that said, "I play the guitar." The lead singer of the band, Billie Joe, also spotted him.

"Hey kid, can you play our songs? If you're serious, then come on up here."

The boy hollered back "Yeah!" and swam his way through all the people, climbing up on stage. He quickly took his place next to the band who handed him a guitar. Together they decided on the next song and a minute later they were jamming.

And get this. Not only could this kid play, he also sang. And he killed it.

He was so good, in fact, that Billie Joe stopped playing the lead and just let the kid riff. He nailed the solo. He was on fire. They played a few more songs together, the band and the crowd loving every minute of it. I bet you're smiling now, too.

Know why?
Cuz he had the moxie to show up that night and go after a dream. And he rocked it!

He took a risk. And he went for it big time by putting it out there for other people to see. And instead of weighing the odds of getting asked to come on stage, which most people would probably say would be slim to none, he went for it anyway.

This is **guts**. It's that **no regrets attitude** I'm talking about. **Where you go for it even when you're not sure what the outcome is gonna be.**

I'd be willing to bet that kid had some major butterflies and was scared at times. But he owned it. He created his rockstar moment with what I'm guessing is one of his favorite bands. On stage. Singing. Performing. Playing the guitar with all he's got. In front of millions of screaming fans cheering him on.

The unexpected bonus? They gave him the guitar to keep.

Way to go kid.

And I know that for my boy Tobin, this was a great example for him to see. Maybe it even sparked him to ask himself, *What do I really want? Am I going for it? How could I put myself out there even more?*

How about you?
What would your sign say?

WOW! YOURSELF

A MINI QUIZ

Everyone has the ability to make a difference, but what that looks like won't be the same for everyone, and that's perfectly alright. Curious about what kind of difference maker you are?

VOILA!

A Mini Quiz just for you.
To help you discover how it is that YOU can change the world.

WHAT KIND OF DIFFERENCE MAKER ARE YOU?

I want to do more good in the world because...

A. I want more purpose in my life

B. I want to make giving a part of my lifestyle

C. I want to make a big impact

Right now ...

A. I'm not sure how I want to make a difference

B. I am passionate about a specific cause or organization

C. I am mission or movement driven

Sometimes I have doubts because...

A. I'm super busy with my work and family. I'm not sure how I'll find the time.

B. I don't have money to donate or the right background I need. Why would anyone trust me to help this cause?

C. I'm all alone. If only I had a team. What can one person really do?

When I think about making a difference I often feel...

A. Unsure of where to start or how to even begin

B. Stuck, overwhelmed, or not confident of what my next steps should be

C. Like I have too much on my plate already—I'm exhausted and afraid of burnout

In my perfect difference-making world I would...

A. Have a list of ideas of ways I could make an impact that would fit into my current lifestyle

B. Feel confident and ready to get started on my cause or mission

C. Feel supported and connected to other difference makers who could help me and keep me going

When I think of doing more to make a difference I feel...

A. Inspired and ready to do something about it

B. Pumped up and a little nervous at the same time

C. Committed to do whatever it takes. OH-YEAH I'm all in!

YOUR RESULTS

Now all you have to do is count up how many of each letter you got to find out what your Heart-Work style is...

Mostly A's: The Kindness Creator

Mostly B's: The Champion

Mostly Cs': The Legacy Maker

These results are designed to help you get your head in the right place. Think of this as your pre-game warm-up. Then in the pages to come, we'll get into creating your personalized plan.

Ready to get a move on? Word.

Let's go!

MOSTLY A'S
THE KINDNESS CREATOR

You want more meaning and purpose in your life. You want to create more positivity and goodness around you, in your home, your neighborhood, and with people who cross your path. You are the Do-Gooder, the Pay-it-Forward person. Kind people are your kinda people.

For the Kindness Creator, heart-work might look like...

- Hiding secret love notes in your neighborhood for people to find
- Bringing in flowers for a coworker when you hear their furry friend passed away
- Holding the door open for a stranger when their arms are full
- Reading to preschoolers during story time at the library a few times a year

Things that might hold you back:
- You're not sure what to do or how to begin
- Sometimes you feel like it's not big enough

PEOPLE iN YOUR POSSE

Your fellow Kindness Creators are your social media friends who post positive photos, feel-good stuff, and pick-me-ups. Or that person in front of you at the café who just bought coffee for the next three people who walk in. Or like, this local guy I read about, JaVonne Hatfield.

DANCiNG HEART GUY

When I saw a photo of a guy holding a huge red heart over his head while dancing on the overpass crossing highway 101 leaving San Francisco, Ooh-la-la I fell in love. More proof that Heart is Hot. I found out via a local news website that he does this twice a week just to make people happy on their morning rush hour commute. How rad is that?!

In an interview with *SF Gate*, JaVonne said, "This is something so simple, but it can do so much to make someone's day. It makes my day. It's all just for the love, just to make people happy." Right on JaVonne!

This is what Revolution Super Love is about.

This is literally HEART-work (pun intended) in action.
Are you falling in love, too?

MOSTLY B'S
THE CHAMPION

You want to make kindness and giving part of your lifestyle. You have a mission or cause you want to support or that you're passionate about. You want to be a part of something bigger. You are the Humanitarian. The Ring Leader. The Community Builder.

For the Champion, heart-work might look like...

- Organizing a charity walk to raise money for a cause you care about
- Volunteering once a week at the after school program or coach a youth sports team
- Putting together a clothing, book, or food drive

Things that might hold you back:

- Feeling stuck or getting overwhelmed with all of your ideas
- You know what you want to do but you're not confident or sure of your next steps. You want the perfect plan to follow

PEOPLE IN YOUR POSSE

Champions are that friend's roommate who teaches a free class every other week on cartooning or hip-hop or gardening to people in their community. Or the awesome guy you follow on Instagram who gives virtual guitar lessons to kids in juvie. Or my huge-hearted friend Michael Bride who started a really cool project called *Operation: Brown Bag Christmas*.

SPREADING HOLIDAY SPIRIT

Michael's goal was to help the homeless and people living on the street in and around his community during the holiday season by delivering to them daily essentials like toothbrushes, toothpaste, deodorant, socks, and gloves, as well as grocery gift cards and fresh food. He added a personal touch to each bag, too—a homemade cookie and holiday card.

Michael invited his friends and local businesses to help out, either by contributing their time, donating a gift to put in the bags, or spreading the word by telling their friends about it. He also set up a Go Fund Me page where people could make a cash contribution or see what items were needed so they could donate those. Then Michael, along with friends and volunteers, loaded up his truck and made the deliveries.

Michael said, "I created this program because I lived on the streets one time and I understood what it can be like and about two weeks before Christmas one year, I was struggling with some work issues, and was feeling sorry for myself, and wondering why I wasn't feeling it. I remembered how good I felt the year before, to forget about myself for a bit, and contribute to others."

Due to powerful word of mouth through social media, that first year, Michael gathered enough supplies to feed over 250 men, women, and children in Snohomish County, WA in one day. Since then, Operation Brown Bag Christmas has continued to grow each year—last year they handed out nearly 1500 bags. How cool is that?!

"Finding the meaning of Christmas is easy," he said. "All you have to do is share it with someone else."

MOSTLY C'S
THE LEGACY MAKER

It's all about IMPACT baby. You want to leave a legacy. You want to change the world. You will invest whatever time it takes. You're in it for the long run. And you might already be started. You are the Activist. The Spokesperson. The Founder. You are devoted, committed, and determined.

For the Legacy Maker, heart-work might look like...

- Becoming a speaker, author, spokesperson, or advocate for a cause

- Starting a nonprofit or making a documentary film

- Volunteering or working to rally for causes you care about as part of your lifestyle. It's something you'll always do

- Raising money, spreading the word, getting others involved in a cause or charity you're passionate about helping in a bigger way

Things that might hold you back:

- You're missing the how-to's and the master plan

- You need help and support when you get stuck

- You want to know how to build community around your mission or cause. You're on the lookout for more people to help you spread the word and do the work

PEOPLE iN YOUR POSSE

When we think of Legacy Makers, a favorite that comes to mind is Dr. Jane Goodall with her admirable dedication to protecting the environment and saving the chimpanzees from extinction. Or author and speaker Josh Shipp, a former at-risk foster kid turned youth advocate who's on a mission to help as many young people as possible.

Or how about all the super cool businesses out there that donate or advocate for a particular cause, like TOMS, which helps a person in need for every product purchased, or Patagonia who is committed to environmental and social responsibility, or The Coffee Oasis that started in my hometown of Bremerton, WA which supports youth programs that provide internships, street outreach, mentoring, shelter, and support to teenagers in need.

I have to tell you about one Legacy Maker I admire; my inspiring friend from college, Angela True. Angela is an incredible example of how one person can use a traumatic event to turn pain into purpose.

VOiCE AGAiNST GUN ViOLENCE

Angela's father was murdered when she was only sixteen years old, and she and her family suffered deeply in the aftermath. Because her mother was ill, Angela and her sibling went into foster care, they lost their horse, their home... their family. Her mother died shortly after. But Angela was determined to not let her father's killer take one more day of her life away.

Angela talks openly about her personal tragedy as she continues to heal through her own journey with PTSD. She uses her voice to advocate and speak up against gun violence and to bring awareness to mental health issues. She writes from the heart. She shares the details. The pain. And the problem with weapons in the wrong hands. She is both courageous and dedicated.

But she doesn't stop there. When Angela learns of another such shooting, she reaches out to the victims' families to offer support and understanding, something she deeply wishes she had. Today she continues to share her journey on social media and is in the process of writing her first book.

This is rallying for a cause. *This* is intentional advocacy. *This* is what leaving a legacy looks like.

KNUCKLES FOR LOVE

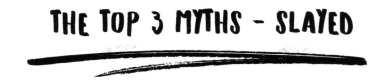

THE TOP 3 MYTHS - SLAYED

**NO ACT OF KINDNESS, NO MATTER HOW SMALL,
IS EVER WASTED**

—AESOP

Before we go any further, I am going to hit the brakes.

You've got a big heart and want to do some good, so before any hesitation or doubt has a chance to creep in, let me slay a few common myths and misconceptions about difference-making.

MYTH #1: i DON'T HAVE ENOUGH TiME

I'm gonna bust this myth right outta the gate.

Learn to say No. Prioritize.
Own the Clock.

You have to make time for the stuff that matters. Did you catch that? You have to do it, because time's not just gonna stop or wait for you. But don't fret. There's always something you can change, move, or shimmy around that will free up your schedule for something you love, value, or want to do more of.

We all have the same number of hours in a day and people all over the world do amazing things with the time they've got. How you spend your time is totally up to you. It's yours. Take control of it. Make it count. Literally.

And let's not forget to mention trying to get that perfect **"life-balance"** thing dialed in.

Oh, uh-huh…*that*.

I used to think a balanced life meant having an equal amount of time every week for all the things I cared about like family, friends, work, exercise, passions, down time, relaxation, and everything else that's important to me. And if I couldn't fit it all in, I'd feel frustrated or exhausted and wonder what was wrong with me.

The struggle finally stopped when I figured out that while having a balanced life is possible, it doesn't often look the way we think it should.

The key to creating balance is to play a game of give and take. **Because maintaining work/life/family balance comes from being present with all of them, just not at the same time.** Did you get that? Seriously. Reread. This is a game changer.

Choose what you do with your time. And once you decide where to spend yours, be where you're at. Go for presence over balance every time.

Fact: We can't go back and get more time. Believe me, I've tried. So take a second to think about how you're spending yours.

Want to say no? Say no!

Need a little help taking things off your plate that you don't want to do? Then I think you're gonna love my #1 favorite tool comin' up!

THE FUCK iT BUCKET

Picture a bucket or (grab a real one). Any size you want. Now imagine it or put it somewhere in your house where you'll see it when you walk by.

Anytime you think of something you wish you could just get off your plate, throw it in the bucket. When you come across something you want to stop doing or want to change, write it down and dump it in the bucket.

What if it's too big to fit? Not a problem. If you're wondering how to put your annoying boss or your ex in there, just write down their name on a piece of paper and toss that baby in.

…S-W-I-S-H!
Alrighty, you're ready. Let's get started.

Grab a pen and paper, set that timer for two minutes, and make a list of all the things you'd love to throw into your Fuck It Bucket. Don't think, just write.

Things like:

- Saying "yes" when I really mean "no." *Fuck That!*

- Picking up my kids' dirty clothes all over the house. *Fuck it!*

- Answering the phone when Negative Nancy calls (again) just to complain. *No Fucking Way!*

- Raising my hand to volunteer one more time for something I really don't want to do, but feel guilty saying "no." *Fuuuuuuck That!*

- Letting the voice in my head tell me I can't do something without giving it a shot. *Absofuckinglutely Not!*

You get the picture. Write them down. Plop them in. And once it's filled up, DUMP that sucker out. That's right! Get rid of it. (Question: Why does it have to be a bucket, Gia? Answer: Duh, because it rhymes.)

"Being busy" gets a bad rap, amiright? But in truth, **being busy isn't bad as long as we're busy with the right things.**

Let's just say I love my flexible lifestyle and I'm really protective of my time. And I've worked hard to learn how to say "yes" only to the things I truly want to do and say "no" to the things I'm no longer excited about or into anymore.

**However, for a while, I felt like something was missing.
Have you ever feel like that?**

For me it centered around *purpose*. I'd been wanting to do more out in the world and there was this one cause I was passionate about, but wasn't sure I had the time to volunteer. But I also knew that deep down I didn't want another six months to go by wishing I'd just jumped in. So I went for it.

But I gotta be honest here. As excited as I was to add this into my life, I was also kinda freaking out on the inside.

MAYBE YOU CAN RELATE...

"Seriously…an eighteen-month commitment? Have you lost it sister?!"
"Do I REALLY have the time? Who am I kidding?!"
"How the heck am I going to make the night trainings work around our family evenings and my son's lacrosse practice?"

I could go on and on, but you get the gist.

Can you guess what I had to do?
Ask for help. Period. *That's it.*
Asking for a hand was all I needed to make this work.

So I reached out to friends to coordinate rides for my kiddo. I moved things around on my schedule to free up some pockets of time. And I talked with my family about why this was so important to me and what the commitment looked like so we were all on the same page and could work it out together.

And you know what?
I did it. It happened.

And you know why?
Because I wanted to do it. I decided to make it work. That's it.

How about you?
Let's imagine for a second that we're hanging out right now. Just you and me.

Talk to me...
Are you busy with the right things? Or are there some things you need to change so you can free up your time for the stuff you really wanna do?

Then say yes.
And commit.
And trust yourself to figure it out.

MYTH #2: i'M NOT A MiLLiONAiRE

No extra funds? No problem. Rest easy.

Making a difference is about being kind, caring about each other, and doing something to help out however you can. You don't have to write a big fat check, make a donation, or put loads of money into the tip jar. And you don't need to raise tons of money to get your gig off the ground, either. (Hello! That's what grants are for!) There are so many things you can do to make a difference that cost absolutely nothing.

Not sure what to do? Hit up the next paragraph.

MYTH #3: i DON'T KNOW WHAT TO DO

If you're chomping at the bit and wanna get started today, like *right now,* and you're feeling a little stumped, here's a kick start quick list for you to get your givin' on with only a little time and money and a whole lotta return.

iF YOU'VE GOT...

30 Seconds: Grab that extra change in your pocket and feed someone's parking meter that's about to expire. Bring your own bag to the market, saving a few trees and your pocketbook. Share a smile. Hug longer.

5 Minutes: Send a few "I'm thinking of you texts" to friends. Register to vote or call your local rep and make your voice heard. Sign up to become an organ donor.

30 Minutes: Shovel the snow in your neighbor's driveway or pick up trash you see on the beach. Next time you're grocery shopping, cruise down the pet aisle and grab a dog toy or kitty treat and drop it off at your local animal shelter on the way home.

60 Minutes: Bake cookies with your kids and then leave them out for the UPS guy with a *"Thanks so much...we appreciate you!"* note attached. Or contact a potential partner organization or investor to set up that coffee date to talk more about your heart-work project.

4 Hours: Skip the Netflix binge and instead outline your business plan or work on your six-month goals timeline. Clean out your closet, your garage, or your bookshelf. Donate. Pass it along.

1 Day a Month: Volunteer at a soup kitchen, food bank, or shelter. Offer your services pro-bono. Help out on your kid's next field trip. Start or finish writing that grant proposal. Take the bus, carpool, or ride your bike to work.

Still not sure where to start? All you gotta do is follow these easy steps:

1. Set the book down for a second
2. Go do something from the list above
3. Give yourself a high-five because you're making it happen
4. Pick the book back up
5. Carry on!

Now that those future excuses and procrastinations are off the table, let's keep movin' and groovin'!

Got more time? Want to do something bigger?

Stay tuned—that's coming up!

HOW DO i CHOOSE JUST ONE? ⚡

If you're wondering how to decide where to start, you're worried about picking just one way to make a difference, or you're not sure how to find the right cause to support, you are not alone. O-M-G I struggled with this one, *big time*. For some reason, I felt like if I just picked one cause, I was somehow ignoring all the rest.

Here's my story of how I finally got past that roadblock and *got started*.

I'd always wanted to go to Africa. To see the country, to meet the people, to experience the culture. I wanted to better understand the immediate needs beyond what I saw on TV.

Finally, through a combination of commitment and determination, I got my chance. There I was, stepping off the plane in Zambia with my friend, Hillary. Not only was my longtime dream finally happening, but unbeknownst to me I was about to meet one of my real life heart-work role models, Angela Malik.

Angela is a beautiful Zambian woman who is as incredible as she is humble and kind. She's the doesn't-take-no-for-an-answer type with a giant heart. She sees a need and does something about it just because it's the right thing to do.

She has spearheaded some incredible give-back programs in and around her community, including a food program to provide meals for orphaned children living on the streets. She's built schools to educate the youth and created jobs for people in the community. She has also started a support group for widowed women, where they can connect and learn about entrepreneurship by making and selling handmade goods. During our three weeks in Africa, my friend and I witnessed Angela in action in many ways.

Angela came into my life at a pivotal time because my plan was to deeply commit to a specific cause when I returned to the U.S. But I wasn't sure which one to choose.

Back home, I had been working with the Humane Society, but I was also feeling a strong pull to help foster children. And because I was a new mother, I had a new passion for families whose children were sick and in and out of the hospital. Lastly, my time in Africa was bringing the challenge of access to clean water to the forefront.

I was overwhelmed. And stuck. *Which one to choose?*

Over tea one evening at Angela's home, I shared a few of my ideas for contributing and told her about my inner struggle. *How do I pick? How do I know which direction to go in? Please, help me decide. Tell me what to do.*

Then I asked her, "How do I choose just one? What if...I choose wrong?

I'll never forget what happened next. She spoke in her calm yet straightforward way, like a wise elder who got to the point quickly:

"You can't choose wrong, Gia."

Then she smiled. With her bright angel eyes.

I so needed to hear that.
(And maybe you do, too.)

Angela told me that when I got home, I should make a list of all the causes I was considering and write down all the reasons why I was drawn to each one. She told me to leave it sitting somewhere, and glance at it every now and then. She told me to keep adding and erasing things on the list as needed. And then see which one stands out the most.

That's exactly what I did.

I made my lists, put them up on my office wall, then added details here and there.

First things first. I wanted to see which organizations were helping create access to clean water. That's when I discovered Scott Harrison (one of my future, imaginary friends) who had just founded Charity: Water, and saw that they had some big plans and serious dedication behind their organization. All I could think was, "Thank YOU Scott and crew!" I felt so relieved (and grateful) to find someone making a difference in this way. I could support them and their mission and cross it off my top priority list.

As I kept walking by my list, I noticed that I was getting pulled toward helping foster children. It made sense really, as my husband and I were in the process of adopting a second child via the foster care system, something we'd always wanted to do.

But the more I learned, through our adoption classes, books, and people I spoke with, the more I couldn't shake the staggering statistics of the number of kids who were stuck in the "system" and needed help in so many ways.

I couldn't believe the lack of advocacy efforts and funding for programs these kids so desperately needed.

I felt like I could do something more. I was at a crossroads. That's when we decided to let our social worker know that we wanted to put our adoption on hold so I could figure out a way to help more kids than just one. I didn't know what I was gonna do or how I was gonna do it, but that was it. Decision made.

A short time later I found myself walking out of the bookstore holding a copy of, *Nonprofit Kit For Dummies* in my hand. My new bible. And eventually, Re:Mix, a creative arts and wilderness retreat for foster youth, was born.

So if you find yourself in that same stuck space I was in, I hope this story saves you time.

Pick One.
Decide.

Don't get caught up trying to pick the "right" cause because there is no such thing. You can't choose wrong if you're following your heart.

DREAM BiG. THEN START SMALL.

We dream big to imagine our biggest desire and hope. To get us excited, to inspire us, to envision what might be possible.

So imagine for a minute.

What's your big difference-making dream right now?
What kind of impact do you want to make?
And if you're going bigger, what do you want your legacy to be?

Allow yourself to go there. **All** the way there.
Kinda scary? Good. That means you're doing it right.

Then we back it up a bit and begin by taking **bite-sized actions** towards that big dream. That way we don't freak out or give fear a chance to stop us from going after it. This is the key to not psyching yourself out.

Keep reading…you've got this.

MOVE AHEAD.

3 STEPS TO GET YOUR HEART ON

IT'S NOT WHERE YOU START, IT'S THAT YOU START.

—JOSH SHIPP

Maybe you're not sure where to start, what to do, or who to help. If only you had some ideas, a mini-plan, and a few action steps to get going. Well my friend, you're in luck...

Off we go!

STEP 01. GET CLEAR
BRAINSTORM

Who do you want to help? Let's get the juices flowing and come up with some ideas for you to pull from.

Grab a piece of paper and your favorite pen or type away on your phone. As the ideas come to you, jot them down. Get ready to play (a.k.a. no over-thinking allowed).

LET'S GO.

1. Which organizations do you support or feel drawn to? Which ones stand out to you? Are there charities or causes that you already like, connect with, or are passionate about? Are there some that you know could use your help? List them out to get warmed up.

Here are a few of my favorites:

Best Friends Animal Society
Homeboy Industries
Surfrider Foundation
The Marine Mammal Center
Montana Wilderness School
Girls on the Run
2020 Mom
CASA: Court Appointed Special Advocate
San Francisco Skate Club
Power of Hope Camp

2. Anything feel like a fit for you now? Let's keep brainstorming. How about your friends or people you admire who do cool give-back work? What do they do? Who do they work or volunteer for? How do they help? Which causes do they support?

Do they volunteer to cuddle with babies, record audio books for the blind or host a toy drive for underprivileged children? Do they give of their time to build homes with Habitat for Humanity or spend a few weeks each summer as a camp counselor for youth burn survivors?

3. Still stumped? Jump on Google. Find out what's out there in your community.

E.g.: Oh My Word! I love the free book libraries that are popping up in neighborhoods. I think it would be really fun to build one.

4. To come at it from a different angle, try chunking all your ideas under different types of heart-work and see what comes to mind.

COMMUNITY

VETERANS

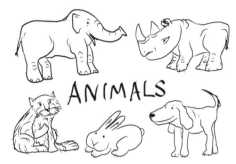

ANIMALS

ENVIRONMENT AND OCEANS

THE ARTS

FUNDRAISING & MICRO LOANS

TEACH MENTOR COACH EDUCATION

HEALTHCARE

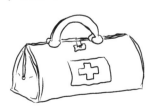

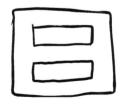

EQUAL RIGHTS

Feel free to use this list and sketch as a guide to help you get started making your own:

Environment: Trees, earth, air, water, preservation, oceans, gardening, glaciers

Animals: Wild (orangutans, elephants), pets (humane society), ocean (whales)

Children: Kids, US/ International (school help, adoption, foster youth, read books, sports, babies), college youth, equal education

Health: Care for everyone, fund a cure (cancer, AIDS, malaria, alzheimers), food, shelter, water, Let's Move (Michelle Obama's campaign), cooking, healthy eating

Sports: (Special Olympics, Boys and Girls Club, athletes on the slopes)

Art: Music, photography, dance

People: Human rights, sex trafficking, eldercare, military, homeless

Business: Micro-loans, teaching skills to everyday people, youth fellowships, mentoring

Local: family, friends, neighborhood, coworkers, mentors, schools

5. When you read something in the news around an important issue or cause in the world, which ones grab your attention the most? Write 'em down.

6. If there was one cause you would be *all in for* if you knew exactly what to do and had no doubts that you could help, what would it be?

Now imagine you're famous or at a party with all the A-listers and you're one of them. What's your give-back "thing"? What are you known for?

My dream give-back gig would be to…
I'd make an impact by…
In a perfect world, I'd leave my legacy by…
If I could just do one thing to make the world a better place it would be…

7. Now look back over your lists. Which ones stand out to you most right now? List them here.

•

•

•

DECIDE. PICK ONE.

This is where you choose something.

Which group/person/cause stands out to you? Which one are you pas-sionate about helping? If you don't know right now, that's A-OK. Just choose one to start with. Be open to the windy path approach…you never know where it's going to lead or who you might meet along the way.

Decide. What leads your heart?
Pick a cause that means something to you personally.

If I was going to do something tomorrow to help I would choose to support _____(name of charity, cause, or organization here)_____.

Whatever you pick, embrace it.

Do it with intention.

Purpose. Passion.

Enthusiasm.

CHECK YO'SELF: HEART- POP'

If you want to do meaningful work in the world that you also love, you have to follow your heart.

That means finding a cause that fires you up and makes your Heart Pop! You know, that feeling you get when you're so excited about making a difference that you literally jump out of bed in the morning and say, IT'S GO TIME people! Or when you think about giving back in this way, your heart is so happy it just might burst. POP!

A friendly reminder: If you or a loved one has battled a disease or experienced something traumatic, that doesn't mean you're dishonoring yourself or them if you choose to make your impact in an unrelated way. You don't need to help a cause just because you understand what someone might be going through. It's much more important that you feel excited and inspired to do the work.

I've struggled with this dilemma myself. I've spent a little over fifteen years experiencing the heartache of memory loss and dementia, starting with my grandmother, and then a few years after she passed, again with my mom. I know I could help people from what I've learned. When I meet someone who's in the same boat, I understand their struggles, fear, and frustrations. Boy, do I get it. I could easily make this my "thing." Yet, it's not what I want to do. Just because I've been through it personally doesn't mean I have to put my stake in the ground for the cause. That doesn't mean I'm not passionate about it or that I don't care, but honestly, it's too fresh for me. I'm still healing. It's not my heart-pop.

Hear this: If you want your passion to be sustainable, you have to do this for you. So if you realize you've put yourself in a corner or edited your ideas based on fear, doubt, or a sense of obligation, it's okay to switch directions or get rid of 'em. PHEW! I can already see that weight lifting off your shoulders. Don't forget, change is always an option.

ViSUALiZE iT

There's a reason why athletes, surgeons, and soldiers use visualization to enhance their performance and help them achieve their goals. When they visualize, they see themselves in their future as if their goal has already happened. They won the gold medal. They performed a flawless operation. They saved lives. And what I love about this technique is that anyone can do it and receive the benefits.

YOU READY TO GET YOUR iMAGiNATiON GAME ON?

Okey. Dokey. We're gonna take a little journey together to imagine what your ultimate difference-making goal, mission, and vision might look like.

For some of you, this is gonna feel a little strange or maybe even unnecessary. If you're thinking, *Gia, seriously I just want to donate blood once a month. I don't need to visualize myself doing it and changing the world one pint at a time*, then feel free to skip this.

For the rest of you, I invite you to join in. Because, this is the super fun part and it can really help with figuring out how to get started. Or maybe you're already on your way but you're ready to do more…to dream bigger. Then I think you'll dig this.

HERE WE GO!

Picture yourself in the future, whatever amount of time feels right for you. Maybe one-to-three years from now. Or maybe you want to dream even bigger so it's like WAY out there—in-the-future-before-I-die-kinda-thing. You decide.

Now that you've got the timeframe figured out, I want you to think about your heart-work. The thing that excites you. Maybe it's your answer to the question from above—*if I could change anything in the world and knew I would succeed, what would I be doing*? Don't forget to throw all of the I-could-nevers out the window.

WHAT DO YOU WANT TO DO?

I want to donate platelets a few times per year and invite my friends to join me.
I want to help train or pair service dogs with veterans.
I want to climb a mountain to raise funds and awareness for suicide prevention.
I want to create art with a purpose by designing products with a message.
I want to raise money for buying trees to plant in my neighborhood.
I want to help with medical research to find a cure for cancer.
I want to regularly offer my services of [insert your skills here] pro-bono.

Fantastic! Now imagine that you're *doing it*. **The goal of visualizing is to help you feel *now* what you want to feel *then*. See yourself there. And picture it as if it's already happened.** (Hint: Sometimes it helps to close your eyes for a minute.)

So…where are you?

What are you doing? Look around. What do you see? What do you hear? What do you smell? Are there other people with you? Are you by yourself?

Or you might like imagining it this way. Step outside yourself and pretend you're watching yourself in a movie. You are the main character, the lead actor. And you're making an impact, in your own magnificent way. (Again, close your eyes.)

What do you see?
What are you doing?
Who are you helping?
Where are you?

And now the most important question— **HOW DO YOU FEEL?**

Are you excited, smiling, happy?
Do you feel free, alive, proud, empowered?

AHHH, THAT'S THE TICKET.

Pay attention to how accomplishing this goal will make you feel, because your feelings will let you know when you're onto something and they can help drive you where you want to go.

62

So, I'm asking again…*how do you feel?*

And for all of our *Mini Quiz Legacy Makers* here, before we move on you might want to give this last exercise a shot:

Imagine you're walking up on stage as the keynote speaker at a fundraising event or you're being honored or receiving an award.

Where are you? Who's in the audience?
What are you saying? And what's your drop-the-mic moment?

Again, *how do you feel?*
(And if it's not too much to ask, can I get your autograph?)

WRITE iT DOWN

Once you've got your vision, write that big dream down as if it's as good as done. Include all the juicy details. What were you doing? What stood out to you or surprised you? Anything specific you want to remember? And don't forget to capture how you feel. Jot it all down.

Or you might like to try writing it out this way: Write a note to yourself from your future self looking back. Or go **Mad Libs style** and fill this out:

Dear Revolution Super Love Rockstar me,

I'm so excited that I'm making a difference by _____

_____(what you want to do)_____

and I can't believe that I _____

_____(something you did)_____.

Only in my wildest imagination would I have guessed I was able to

_____(another thing you accomplished)_____.

And you're never gonna guess who just emailed me about

_____(something coming up that you're excited about)_____!

Can you believe _____

_____(a person, organization or media company you admire)_____

emailed me?!! Eeek! And you know what else? _____

___(one more awesome thing about your heart-work that's going on)___.

Yep, that happened too. And I couldn't feel anymore_____

_____(positive feeling or feelings)_____

if I tried. I just wanted to let you know that big things are on your hori-

zon and I've got your back.

Sincerely,
Your future self

Kinda fun, huh?! Remember, with our bigger dreams we write 'em down to help us imagine where we're going and how we want to feel once we get there. And in a bit we'll break this big thing apart, piece by piece, so you can get started taking small steps toward making it happen.

STEP 02. MAKE A PLAN

SWEET! You've decided on what cause you'd like to begin with, you have your big vision of where you'd like to go, and now you're ready for the next step. It's time to make a mini-plan. Remember when we talked about Dream Big and Start Small? This is the start small spot.

LIST IT.

You've pinpointed your cause. Check! Now it's time to brainstorm some ideas about what you might like to do for that cause. Write down *all* the possibilities that come to mind. Think details, details, details. Sometimes it helps to think of a short timeline, like over the next few weeks or months. What would you like to do? And what do you think you might need to do to move forward? List it.

Here are two examples:

I want to do something to help _____RESCUE ANIMALS_____.

Maybe I could...

Walk dogs, pet cats, snuggle with bunnies, help with adoption days, fund-raisers, outreach, offer support with my marketing skills or grant writing, event planning, help spread the word, join the board, or collect donations.

I want to do something to help _____ DOMESTIC VIOLENCE

SURVIVORS _____.

Maybe I could...

Answer phones on a hotline, work at a shelter, collect supplies and donations, do educational outreach, offer training, or teach a class at the shelter.

NOW iT'S YOUR TURN.

I want to do something to help_____.

Now make a list of all the things you might like to do for this cause. Anything goes.

-
-
-
-
-

MY TOP 3

Now that you've got a list going, we're going to prioritize it a bit. Check out what you wrote down and choose a few you'd like to look into further.

My Top 3 ideas I'd like to explore are:

1.

2.

3.

Example: I want to find out more about...

1. Walking dogs
2. Helping at adoption days
3. Community outreach and spreading the word about the organization

BREAK ONE DOWN

Now you're going to choose one idea from above to start with and break it down into smaller steps. What will you need to *do* in order to make that idea happen?

The idea I'd like to start with is _____.

What steps might I need to do to make this happen? Break it down into 5 smaller steps.

1.

2.

3.

4.

5.

Examples:

The idea I'd like to start with is ___HELPING WITH ADOPTION DAYS___.

What steps might I need to do to make this happen?

1. Sign up for volunteer orientation.
2. Attend orientation.
3. Find out when they hold adoption days, as well as which days I'm available.
4. Find out what type of specific help is needed with the adoption days.
5. Find out if I need any additional training to work directly with the animals.

SCHEDULE iT. (put a ~~ring~~ date on it)

You've got a list. You broke it down. Now it's time to pull out your calendar and assign a due date for each step so you remember what action you need to take to hit your goal. (Don't skip this step!)

Example:

April 14: Look up on the website to find out when adoption days are held and figure out if I'm available.

April 15: Call the adoption organization and ask my questions. (Do they need people to drive animals to the event? Do they need volunteers to contact foster families to make sure they're coming or dropping off their foster pet? Do they need people to pass out information to interested adoptees? Do I need any additional training to work directly with the animals?)

April 16: Sign up for the volunteer orientation.

April 26: 7:00 pm—Attend orientation.

CHECK YO'SELF

Make a plan. But remember that plans are just plans—they can and will change. Nothin' has to be set in stone. You can always re-decide. Be open to shifting things as needed, and remember that it's fine to change your mind along the way.

METANOIA (n.) the journey of changing one's mind, heart, self, or way of life

It was January and I wasn't where I wanted to be. I was panicked and stressed. A year had past since I'd filed the paperwork for my non-profit for foster youth, Re:Mix. I'd raised money, received grants, found a program director, built relationships with social service agencies, and told everyone that we'd be launching our very first retreat that summer. The word was out. There were even articles in the paper. Things were happening, which was amazing. But at the same time, it felt too rushed.

We weren't ready. I could only move so fast. I'd put all of me into it and I was committed to getting it right. I wanted a full group of kids who were stoked to come. I wanted social worker support. I wanted talented, committed, amazing staff, guides, and teachers. I knew it wasn't time, but my strategic plan said that it was. I was supposed to start in less than four months. And I had made a promise to so many people. I felt stuck.

After one of my many meltdowns to my guy, he said in his calm-to-my-crazy way, "Gia, you're the one creating this. You're the one doing most of the work, volunteering your time, and being a fulltime mom. If you aren't feeling it and you don't feel ready, then change the start date."

69

He said it so matter-of-factly. Like it was a no-brainer.

"People will understand. Just keep them in the loop like you do, let them know what you're up to and when the new projected launch date will be, and you'll be good to go."

So I did. I listened to what I knew I needed to do. I changed my mind. I changed the plans. And I waited one more year to kick it off. I raised more money, got more community support, landed another grant, found an awesome group of foster kids who were excited to come, and hired the perfect people to run it.

And you know what?

No one was upset or ever questioned me. They continued to support the organization and spread the word. The funders and grant organizations understood too, as they know it's part of the startup world.

So make a plan. And know it might change.
Everything's as it's supposed to be.

STEP 03. ACT

Goals are cool, but actually *doing* things is what makes them real. You've got the plan. You know what you want to do. You're right on track. Now it's time to take the plunge and set your goals into action. 3-2-1 we're jumping in!

JUST ONE

You've got your list of ideas for possible next steps, right? Now ask yourself, ***What's one step I can do today to start heading in that direction?*** Think micro-movement here.

Pick one thing.
Write it down.
Yes, now.
(I'll wait.)

Write out a one-sentence (or even a few words) description. Short. Specific. (Hint: Save the world is a little too broad. I tried it already.)

How about something like:
Tell my son/daughter I love them tonight when they walk in the door.
Set up a meeting with my friend who works for that really cool nonprofit to find out how I can get involved.
Send my advocacy piece to the paper for possible publication.

BABY STEP THAT BAD BOY

Now it's time to take that **one BABY step** and put it into action. (Find a step that you know you can accomplish easily.)

Start somewhere.
Do something.
Anything.
Just begin.

Go for it.

Try what I call "What about Bob?" style.

Have you ever seen the movie, "*What About Bob*?" starring Bill Murray?

Baby step to the door.
Baby step past your desk.
Baby step to the elevator.
I'm doing it!!!

If not, you gotta Google "baby steps *What about Bob* elevator scene" and push play. You'll never baby step the same again. I promise. And if Bob can do it, so can you. Once you start baby stepping, the overwhelm will begin to disappear and the path will start to show.

NiGHT LiST

You're moving forward. You're taking small steps of action. And you'll soon find out there are more things to do than you can get to. That means it's time to start making a *night list*. Think of it as your mini-action plan for the next day.

All you gotta do is write down your top three things you're going to do tomorrow before you go to bed each night. Not *want to do*, *need to do*, or *hope to do,* but three things you are GOING to do. Remember— these are baby step things. Simple, easy, check-off-able.

We all know the list could go on and on forever—that's why you're gonna just pick a few and make sure at least one is a baby step toward your heart-work. Of course you can always do more if you wanna, but your goal here is to make sure you GET the TOP 3 DONE.

Heart-Work Night List Examples:

1. Hit the thrift store on the way home from work and drop off our family's donation.
2. Read pages 1-10 of the manual for the hospital volunteer orientation coming up next week.
3. Call 3 donors and thank them for their contribution.

Everything else you accomplish is a bonus, kinda like the icing on the cake!

Want to take it one step further to make sure you get the most important things done and make time for the things that matter? Whip out your calendar for tomorrow and plug in the things you have to do first. Then add in your Night List stuff. And you're all set to go!

CHECK iT OUT:

Morning workout: 6:00am
Kids drop off: 8:00am
Call the power company about bill: 12:00 (lunch break)
Night List #1: Read pages 1-5 of volunteer manual for hospital orientation: 12:15
Pick up kids: 4:00pm
Night List #2: Drop off items at thrift store on the way home
Dinner: 6:30pm
Night List #3: Read pages 6-10 of volunteer manual for hospital orientation: 8:00pm

FUN-iFY iT!

Do I get a shiny green star?

I'd do anything—take out the trash, wash the dishes, pushups, practice the piano—for a green star.

I loved them!

A happy sticker that says, "Yes, You did it!"
Job complete.

As a little girl, I was all about the stars on our chore chart or the super fun stickers I'd get at gymnastics or the stamps my teacher would give me for doing my homework or helping out.

Who am I kidding? I'm *still* all about the green stars and smiley stickers. In fact, there are literally sheets of them right now in my upper right desk drawer. I love to pull them out when I don't feel like doing something or if I'm working toward a goal and want a way to measure my progress as I go.

These visual reminders show me how the little steps I'm taking all add up to the big picture. And it's so much more fun to look at a list with fun stickers on it rather than a bunch of things crossed off, don't you think?

WANNA PLAY? HERE'S HOW.

Write down your goals or list of tasks. (You just did that, right?)
Go do them.

One by one.

When you're done with an item, slap a star sticker next to it.
BAM!

Instant satisfaction!

Then exclaim out loud…YAHTZEE! I got a green star!

What's that? Green stars and happy stickers don't do it for you? No problem. All you gotta do is come up with your own fun way to celebrate, reward, and acknowledge what you're getting done. Whatever floats your boat, have at it.

PUT iT ALL TOGETHER

The key is to keep moving forward even if you don't know what ALL the next steps are going to be. This is a process. A system. A mini-plan to get you going. It's not meant to be concrete. You can change your ideas or steps as you learn more. It's just a way to get you from *I think I wanna* to *I'm doing it*.

If you're a visual learner or an organizational fanatic like me, you might like putting things together like this where X marks the spot you want to go—**TREASURE MAP** style. There are goal markers and step lines there for you to fill out however you want to.

You can also set the time frames. Again—this is your treasure map. Do you want to see quick results? Then maybe your map is weekly with a baby step each day. If you're more motivated by three- or six-month planning, then create your map accordingly.

You can fill it out ahead of time or as you go. Whatever works for you.

My goal is to...and I want to do it by...(date).
By ___**December 7th**___ I want to check off this...

Break it down: It's time to break your **GOAL** down by building in some checkpoints along the way.

Fill in three goals for each time period below.

During **week 1** I did this . . .
This week (#2) I will . . .
Next week (#3) I want to . . .
After **one month (#4)** of working towards my goal to help this cause I want to . . .

Six months from now, what would you like to have accomplished? What would you most like to gain?

One year from now I want to . . .

CHECK YO'SELF

The only way to make an impact is to start taking action. Thinking about doing something isn't the same as actually doing it. You have to begin. Start somewhere. Pick one action step you could take right now. And go do it.

MARIO'S PLAYGROUND ⚡

Years ago, I was at a conference for a values-driven skincare company I was working for when the guest speaker said something that caught my attention. She told us to think about one goal. Just one thing we wanted to accomplish. Then she told us to write down one step we could take toward making it happen. That's it.

It was a great exercise, except for one problem. We were supposed to be focusing on things like how much money we wanted to make per month or how many customers we wanted to book or who we could invite to grow our team, but I was feeling a pull to do something that could have a much bigger impact in the world.

My mind was elsewhere because of a recent tragedy that had happened in our town. A four-year-old boy named Mario had been killed while riding his Big Wheel in front of his house because there was nowhere safe to play. Ever since hearing the news, I'd been wondering what I could do to help. *But what does this have to do with my work*, I wondered. *Maybe I could somehow use my business to do something?*

There it was, I had a goal. Figure out how I could help Mario's family. I knew it wasn't business-related (yet), but it was what I cared about at that moment, so I wrote it down. And my one step? Call the local paper that ran the story to find out more.

So that's what I did.

With just one phone call, I found out that by publishing this story they were hoping to raise awareness and funds to help the kids in Mario's neighborhood with the possibility of building a playground. So I knew what my next steps were—I could spread the word. Easy. And I decided I could help raise money by donating my commission from my product sales. I was on it!

I sent an email out to my friends and customers and shared Mario's story. I explained why I wanted to help, and what I wanted to do, then gave them a few ideas of how they could join me. The response was incredible. Once they heard Mario's story, so many of them wanted to pitch in.

My plan was off to a great start, but I couldn't stop thinking about Mario's family. I couldn't even begin to imagine what it would be like to lose a child. I decided to try to do something just for his mom. So I reached out to my local paper connection again to see if they could touch base with Mario's mother to let her know I wanted to host a spa day just for her and anyone she wanted to invite. She said yes.

Two months after that professional development conference where the idea of helping Mario's family first began to form, I walked into the community center that had kindly donated the space for the day. There, Mario's mother, and her family and friends, were waiting for me.

Though I'd hosted many events like this in the past, I was feeling a little nervous, in part because I really wanted Mario's mom to have a great afternoon, and in part because of the language barrier (she spoke Spanish and I don't). Thankfully, my beautiful friend Marnie offered to come along to translate and help out.

Toes dipped in the warm water and smiles began to brighten. And even though we spoke different languages, it didn't really matter— compassion is understood in every language. The afternoon was incredible. Even though this had been such a dark time in the lives of these women, on that day there was so much joy in the room. I was grateful to be a part of it.

When I left, I hugged everyone goodbye. I gave Mario's family a check for the money we raised and when I got home I sent a quick email to my community to let them know how thankful his family was for our collective kindness.

I was blown away by how taking just one step toward a goal had snowballed into something I couldn't have imagined if I tried. Before I knew it, I was off and runnin' toward a new more meaningful business model that I'd created without even realizing it. I ended up spending the next few years using my business as a tool to raise money to help people and causes I cared about. And it all started by answering one question.

So now it's my turn to ask you...

What's **one goal** you want to achieve through your heart-work?
And now, the magic ingredient, what's **one step** you can take today toward doing that?

Really, you've got nothing to lose.
The world awaits.

WHAT iF...

We hugged instead of hated.
We rallied for love instead of protesting in rage.

What if...
We stopped asking what's wrong with the world and paid more attention to what's right.

What if...
We used our voice instead of staying silent.
We decided to do something about the stuff that fires us up or speaks to our heart.

What if...
Our actions made kindness the norm, not the exception.

iMAGiNE iF...

We all said hello, thank you, and I love you.

Imagine if...
We knew our neighbors, the mail carrier, and the guy selling newspapers on the street.

Imagine if...
We all decided to reach out or help one another when we knew there was something we could do.

Imagine if...

We were grateful not for just the day but for each moment.

Imagine if...

We all lived the way we want to be remembered.

Imagine if...

We all felt loved, safe, and cared for and had somewhere to belong.

iMAGiNE iF...

We did it together.

WHAT iF...

We did it together.

Creating community AROUND A CAUSE

IF YOU WANT TO GO FAST, GO ALONE.
IF YOU WANT TO GO FAR, GO TOGETHER.
—AFRICAN PROVERB

One of the best and fastest ways to get started with your heart-work is by creating or connecting with community, hands down. And by community I mean a group of people who come together for a common purpose or goal.

i LOVE THiNKiNG ABOUT COMMUNiTY iN TERMS OF 'HOODS.

Neighborhoods.
Sisterhoods. Brotherhoods.

It's got such a feel-good vibe around it, doesn't it?

Cue music!

"Who are the people in your neighborhood, in your neighborhood, in your neigh—bor—hood! Oh, who are the people in your neighborhood, the people that you meet each day . . ." Remember this little ditty from *Sesame Street*? Where Big Bird, Cookie Monster, Mr. Snuffleupagus, and friends cruise around the neighborhood singing and saying hello and good morning to their neighbors?

Kinda gives you the warm fuzzies, right?

There's something about hangin' with like-minded people, where you can show up and just be yourself. You don't have to explain anything if you don't want to, because the people *get you*. Communities are powerful and necessary sometimes.

Other than those warm fuzzies, **here are four reasons why embracing community is so important:**

No.#1: To create awareness around your cause, spread the word faster, and educate
No.#2: To connect like-minded people around your mission or cause
No.#3: To raise money for your cause, mission, or organization
No.#4: To get ideas, support, and connect with people like you

Pretty freakin' great, right!?
Who doesn't want some of that??

Let's dive in real quick here and explore how you can leverage community to get in on all that goodness.

#1 CREATE AWARENESS. EDUCATE. SPREAD THE WORD.

One incredible way to raise awareness, educate, and spread the word about what you're passionate about is to create community around a cause or common goal. You see examples of this everywhere and you've noticed, haven't you? That's because they're effective.

You know, like charity walks or cycling for a cure. For example...

Relay for Life (American Cancer Society)
Walk to End Alzheimer's (Alzheimer's Association)
Ride to End AIDS (AIDS/LifeCycle)
Step Out Walk to Stop Diabetes (American Diabetes Association)
Harley-Davidson Ride for Life (Muscular Dystrophy Association)
Best Buddies Challenge (Best Buddies International)

Or perhaps you've spread the world or attended an event to promote awareness, advocacy, or raise money for causes like these:

World Autism Awareness Day
This is my Brave (ending mental health stigma through story)
Girls on the Run
National Foster Care Month
Be the Match (The National Marrow Donor Program®)
The Red Shoe Ball (The Ronald McDonald House Charity)
Habitat for Humanity
Breast Cancer Awareness Month
MADD (Mothers Against Drunk Driving)
Buckle up for Life Campaign

Or maybe you've read about or were a part of advocacy events like The Women's March, Black Lives Matter, the protests at Standing Rock, Freedom to Marry, DC Climate March, or Earth Day.

Whether you're looking to get involved, connect, or create your own community, getting started is easy. Once again, Google is your new BFF. All you gotta do is type in what you're interested in finding community around and Ka-ZAM!—thousands of results in seconds. You can discover if there are already communities centered around your cause in your area or check out some favorites that you've seen or you took part in in the past to get inspiration. Take some time to think about what made these walks, runs, rides, or events so special.

#2 CONNECTING WITH PEOPLE AROUND A CAUSE: 2 WAYS

// iN REAL LiFE //

Maybe you're more focused on connecting to people around your mission or cause?

You can find your like-minded soul sisters or brothers a couple different ways. IRL (In Real Life) communities come in all shapes, flavors, and sizes. We talked about advocacy events, campaigns, and charity walks already.

In-person communities also happen in or around your hometown. Or maybe you create, attend, support, or rally a community around an existing cause through an in-person retreat, event, workshop, gathering, or hangout.

NOVEMBER 15TH, 2013

Two helicopters were flying overhead and people from all over the Bay were everywhere on the streets of San Francisco. No, Beyoncé wasn't in town and it wasn't The Giants World Series parade...nothing like that. It was better.

People were gathering because the city of San Francisco was invited by the Make-A-Wish Foundation to **help out a five-year old boy named Miles, who was battling leukemia, make his wish to become BATKID come true.** And we all wanted to be a part of it.

Check this out.

Miles kicked off his day by hearing a breaking news story that the San Francisco Police Chief was looking for him because the city needed his help. He answered the call along with his adult Batman partner and, you guessed it, they were off to save the city in their Batmobile.

Batkid had a packed day committing acts of heroism left and right, from saving a damsel in distress who was tied to the cable car tracks and stopping The Riddler from robbing a bank vault to making sure the villain Penguin didn't capture The Giant's mascot Lou Seal! Miles' day ended at City Hall where he was awarded a key to the city from the Mayor in front of thousands of cheering fans.

We were a part of a huge crowd of volunteers, donors, and supporters, many of whom were dressed up as superheroes themselves, who showed up at City Hall to cheer him on and say THANK YOU! Emotions were high. You could literally feel the love. And at one point my son Tobin looked over at me with a beaming smile and said, "Mom, I'm so happy we're here." I still get goosebumps remembering this moment.

I wish I could put into words what it was like to stand there with a group of strangers who had all come together to help a little boy make his wish come true.

And honestly, it was so much more than that. We were also there to support Miles' mother, father, and little brother (Batkids sidekick Robin, of course!) and all of the other families who are fighting daily to keep their children alive. I can't imagine what that would be like.

Someone who wasn't able to be there asked me if Miles looked happy. And my reply was, YES! He was so stinkin' cute! He looked like he was having so much fun. I'm sure he was probably exhausted, but he just kept smiling and pumping his fist to show the crowd his spirit and appreciation.

As of Nov 2017, SF Gate states that Miles is healthy and doing great, as is his family, which is a little larger now that Miles' younger brother Ben recently came into the world.

This is what creating community around a cause IRL can look like.

// ONLiNE //

You can also use online platforms to reach out even further to connect with your people.

Online communities—communities created via the Internet, through podcasts, or on social media platforms like Facebook groups, Instagram, or YouTube— are popping up everywhere. And the reason why these are so great is because distance, time, and money just aren't an issue. That's right. We can connect and rally and support one another no matter where we live. Pretty rad, right?!

Did you know that you can literally search and find a community around almost *anything* you care about, are passionate about, or want to find more about? We're talking anything from obscure communities (knitting beanies for twenty-somethings or urban goat lovers) to more common groups that fall under categories like healthy lifestyles or entrepreneur adventurers or sports fans of specific teams. There are also a ton of support communities based around health issues, like diabetes support groups, or causes, like grassroots activism. The options are endless.

How can you use this though? Let's peek at TiLT Parenting for example.

My amazing friend Debbie Reber founded TiLT to be a community to help parents raising differently-wired kids to do so from a place of confidence, connection, and peace. She created it out of her own personal need and desire to find support and connect with families like her own.

Debbie knew there were so many valuable conversations that were needed and could be shared, as well as so many great resources out there but they weren't all together in one location. So she did something about it. And TiLT Parenting was born.

Through TiLT, Debbie offers information and support for her rapidly growing global community via her personal weekly emails, a Facebook group, her high-ranking podcast that her awesome son Asher sometimes co-hosts, and her manifesto disguised as book Differently Wired: Raising an Exceptional Child in a Conventional World.

Once you start checking out different types of online communities that exist, you'll quickly learn that they each have their own way of sharing information, offering support, and creating space to connect. Some offer tips, how to's, online classes, podcasts to listen to, radio show interviews, meditations, meal plans, and online meet–ups. The list goes on.

Use this for inspiration.

What parts speak to you? How can you bring pieces of what you see online to your own heart-work?

#3 GET MONEY: RAISE FUNDS

Curious about how to use community to raise funds for your cause? Let's get those wheels spinnin'!

If you want to raise funds for your cause, the easiest place to start is your own community. Friends, family, neighbors, online. Do you remember school fundraisers? Selling chocolate, build-your-own pizza kits, wrapping paper, magazine subscriptions. And let's not even get started with Girl Scout Cookies. Yummo...Thin Mint city!

Whose door do our kids go knockin' on to sell their goods? Yup, they start with the people they know. Tap into this. Your network. It's your community. Don't be afraid to ask. These are your people.

A common trend on Facebook or other social media sites is rallying your crew to pitch in for a cause you care about by pledging or donating your special day.

"Hey friends! Instead of buying me a gift or drink at the bar this year for my birthday, I'm inviting you to donate to my favorite cause instead!" Brilliant!

This is a fantastic way for your friends and family to celebrate you by pitching in as a group for something more meaningful. Honestly, how many pairs of unicorn socks, *ahem, excuse me,* I mean, scented candles and mustache trim kits, does one really need? Yeah, I'm talking to you.

Thanks to crowdfunding campaigns and fundraising platforms such as GoFundMe, Generosity, Kickstarter, Indiegogo, or Kiva, we can get the word out, share our story, and start bringing in the money in a matter of days. So hop onto any of these sites or ones like 'em, take a look around, and see what inspires you.

#4 FiND PEOPLE LiKE YOU

Certainly not the least (and maybe even the most) important reason why community is so integral to difference-making superstars is that it helps you find other people like you.

Take support groups—there are millions of them out there, from local to online, and in all different sizes. They exist to bring people together who have been through or are going through something similar, and once you find the right one to connect with, it can make a huge, positive impact on your life.

Cool. So now are you sold on the importance of community but aren't sure where to start? Try this.

It's time to **B.Y.O.C.** (Build Your Own Community)

What are you passionate about? What types of people would you like to connect with? Entrepreneurs? Coaches? Writers? Activists? Sports enthusiasts? Survivors? Athletes? Hobbyists?

Here are a few prompts to help you get going...

I really want to connect with more people who like to_____.
If only I could find some support with _____.

I wish I knew more people who overcame or are going through _____
_____ just like me to connect with.
I am excited to find more about _____.

Google them. Search Facebook, Twitter, Instagram, ask friends. Before
you know it, you'll start building your own community (or maybe you'll
even start your own).

THE 12TH MAN ⚡

As a native Washington girl who grew up with a dad who was both a
high school teacher, counselor, and the football coach, let's just say
clipboards with X's and O's were always lying around our house and
Sunday Night Football was a regular part of my life. Our home team?
The Seattle Seahawks.

Any Seahawks fans here? Give me a Shout! WOOP! WOOP!

Whether you're a fan or not, if you know anything about football or are
connected to friends who do, you're probably aware of the 12th man.
If not, I'll explain. Because the 12th man is a perfect example of what
creating community can look like.

Check out what this started...

**Today it's not just about the names of the players on the field—it's
also about the community that surrounds them.** The Fans. Or what
the Seahawks call, the 12th man. You see, there are eleven players on
the field at a time, and **#12 is YOU.**

Now with number 12 in the mix, you become more than a fan—you're a part of the team. A collective team. And anyone else who's wearing the number 12 is with you.

And you know what that does for a city? For the players? For a team? To feel like the fans are right there with you, cheering you on hardcore, we're talking all in, hair dyed blue and green, bare-chested with the #12 painted on their belly. That's right. You get FIRED UP!

Think about it.

You're out and about rockin' your Seahawk-colored sneaks and you pull into a gas station to fill up. You step out of your car and the guy next to you sees the number 12 on your shirt.

GO HAWKS! he yells.
GO HAWKS! you holler back.

BOOM.
Instant connection.

It doesn't matter if you exchange numbers, meet up to tailgate on the next game day, or never see each other again. You had an "I get you" moment. All because you both root for the same team. You are "on" the same team...the 12th man.

AT
DAWN
WE GIVE

STAND OUT + REACH OUT

THE END RESULT OF KINDNESS IS
THAT IT DRAWS PEOPLE TO YOU.

—ANITA RODDICK

It's almost time to reach out and create more connections, but before you hop on your horse and ride off into the sunset, let's make sure you're ready to cowboy up and BRING IT!

Do I hear a YEE-HAW?! YEE-HAW!

Are you ready to draw more people in to you and your cause? Yes siree! Are you ready to fire people up to pitch in, spread the word faster, help out, or care more? 10-4! Are you ready to make a bigger impact, raise more money, and have tons of fun along the way?

Silly me, of course you are.

Because mediocre ain't part of the Revolution Super Love way, **I'm gonna share with you my top three tips on how to help your cause stand out and be memorable.**

You Ready?
Let's count 'em down.

GIDDY UP!
(Too much cowboy? Said no country girl ever...)

HOW TO STAND OUT TIP NO. #3: PICK YOUR VIBE

Check yourself out…

Hey, you sexy cat lookin' back at me in the mirror: H-O-L-L-A!! Yeah, we know you got it going on, but that's not what I'm talking about here.

What I mean is, **how do you show up in the world? What energy do you put out there? What attitude do you offer?** Are you, a glass half-full or half-empty kinda guy/girl?

And now onto the second and MORE important follow-up questions:

How do you **WANT** to show up in the world? What attitude or perspective do you **WANT** to share with the people around you or in your presence?

IS WHO YOU ARE NOW AND WHO YOU WANT TO BE ONE AND THE SAME?

You can be honest.
This isn't a test.

If the answer is…"*Yes! They're the same!*" you're all set! Keep on rockin' it like you do.
If the answer is…*No.* No sweat! Today's your day. All you gotta do is turn it around.

Perhaps you want to be more of a Happy Hunter or a Go Get 'em

Gabriella or a Kickass Kirk? Right on! It's your call. But don't waste time beating yourself up or looking for excuses if you're not where you wanna be yet. It's all good because maybe your old vibe served its purpose.

The important thing is, you've decided it's time for a shift. SWEET!

Here's what's up.

Standing out *effectively* with heart-work isn't just about what you do—it's also about how you choose to show up. Remember—we like to engage with people who have positive energy because it's welcoming, inviting, and refreshing. It's contagious. We're inspired by people who focus on finding a solution, not just the problem. In other words, we like to be around people who bring good vibes. You know, you've seen these message on T-shirts:

Choose yours. Pick your Vibe.
Be Deliberate.
It makes all the difference.

HOW TO STAND OUT TiP NO. # 2: WALK YOUR TALK

This one's super simple.
Do what you say you're gonna do. Go first.

If you ask others to pitch in, make sure you're doing the same. Want someone to make a donation to your cause? Write the first check. Promise a specific result? Follow through. Don't ask anyone to do what you're not willing to. Make your word mean something.

Walk your Talk.

It creates trust.
Trust creates loyalty.
Loyalty creates community and support for you and your cause.

Get it? Got it? Good.

And now for **my #1 Tip that will make you Stand Out that most people** (but not you) **forget to do…**

HOW TO STAND OUT TIP NO. #1: SAY THANK YOU

This is one of the easiest ways to create a connection, build community, and rally support.

Say…
Thank You.

Write a card. Put a stamp on it. Pop it in the mail.

When someone shares their time with you, **thank them.** When someone donates their money to your cause, **let them know you appreciate their support.** When your community rallies with you around your cause, **thank them.**

As you're working toward your goal, keep the people who are supporting you (donors, clients, family, friends, community) informed along the way. Remember they're here because they want to be part of what you're doing. You can keep them in the loop by letting them know what you're up to and thanking them as you go. And after you complete your program, event, or campaign or hit your goal, don't forget to share your results with the people who supported you. Snap a photo. Send it.

Thank you so much....
We couldn't have done this without your help.

Thank you for being a part of our beginning.
Without your generous support this wouldn't have happened.

Look what we did together.
I can't thank you enough.

Gratitude. Appreciation. Acknowledgment.
Love bombs go a long way.

DON'T SKIP THIS.

REACH OUT

If you want to build community or get others involved with your heart-work, you have to be willing to tell people what you're doing or creating, sometimes even before you feel ready, and maybe even before it exists...GASP! What'ch you talkin' bout Willis?!

By that I mean, **start talking.**

When we say it out loud, to ourselves first and then with others, it starts to feel real and come alive. And ooooh baby does that feel good.

The good news? When you feel passionate, driven, or excited about what you're working on or doing, reaching out is no big thing. Remember: the goal is to invite people to help you and your mission or cause and let them know why you care.

When you dare to share and put yourself out there, I promise you will start to make connections with your kinda people. The word will spread. The momentum will build and more good will happen.

MAKE iT PERSONAL

We want to know.

What's **your** story and why do **you** care?

Why do you volunteer each week to tutor elementary school kids during your lunch break?
Why are you so devoted to criminal justice reform?
Why are you so excited to help with the Special Olympics this summer?
Why do you coach, teach, mentor, share, volunteer, advocate for...

What's **your** reason for doing what you do? Make it personal.

Here's why.

Genuinely sharing your own story gives those who hear it the opportunity to connect with you. And when they understand where you're coming from and why you stand for your cause, they'll lean in to listen more.

Because it's where the emotion is. The heart. This is where the passion lives.

And Passion Persuades.
And brings us together.
And inspires us.

So no need to be shy. This is your opportunity to get personal and share that energy and enthusiasm that drives you. That spark you've got? It's contagious.

And once we hear more, then we know how to help you, support you, or spread the word. This is how you create possible donors, involved advocates, and friends. We love helping people we know and care about, but you've got to tell them what you're up to first.

Remember that this is different from sharing the mission of the organization you support. This is your personal reason for being here and why you're doing what you do.

SCRIPT iT. OWN iT. RUN WiTH iT.

Need a little more help? Not sure what to say when people ask what you do?

Wanna know how to say it with confidence?

No worries, I've got you.

Do this.

SCRiPT iT.

1. Write it down.

Let's say you run into an old friend at the grocery store and they say, *Hi* (insert your name here) *how's it going, what are you up to these days?* What would you say? Write down your phrase as it would be today.

I'm working on / involved with / excited about / putting together / looking into…. (your cause).

I help / advocate / teach / speak / write for / support…(what you do) so *that…*(why you care).

Ex: *I advocate and create positive change for new mothers and families so that they can live amazing, healthy lives together.*

2. Short & Sweet.

The intention of the phrase is exactly that. It's a "phrase" not a paragraph or a three-minute spiel. It's just a teaser of what you're working on to share, connect, and spark interest. Keep playing with it until it sounds juicy and fun.

3. Say it out loud.

Again, pretend your friend asked you this question and practice saying it out loud. I know it might feel a little silly at first, but this really works. Say it a few times. Do you like what you hear? How does it feel?

Go ahead and keep tweaking your phrase until you capture the feelings you want. The key is that it feels exciting and perfect for you…because when it does, it will come across naturally.

OWN iT

Now that you've hammered down the phase you wrote above, I want you to own it, my friend. Own what you're doing and why you're here.

We don't want to hear any wishy washy replies like, *I'm thinking of... maybe trying to start something... But I'm not really sure... because I don't really know how...*

Instead **OWN IT!**

You've gotta have confidence in yourself and what you're working on. If you don't, it's gonna be hard for others to jump on board with you. Speak with passion and no fear. Share it with others because it matters to you. Trust me—your heart-work is real and worth it.

So real quick, let's revisit question number 1 where you're at the grocery store, and *this time* I want you to try saying your phrase with some serious **own-it-ness** added in.

Ready, Set...Go!

Your strong belief in your vision and the way you share it is gonna be key to moving forward and connecting with others.

Next: *Practice. Practice. Practice.*

Perfecto! Now that you're comfortable saying your phrase out loud, practice sharing it with friends or family or people you trust until it feels natural. Don't be surprised if you go back and edit/tweak some more after you've shared it a few times. (Just be sure that the reason you're changing it is because *you* want to make it feel more authentic, not because someone else told you to. Your gut will let you know when it's right.)

It's easy to own it.
You can do this, without a doubt.

All you have to do is confidently state what you're working on, even if you don't have it all figured out yet. (It's okay, you're not supposed to.)

RUN WiTH iT

Now that you're ready to talk about your vision, let's put it to use. The best and fastest way I've found to get up and runnin' with your heart-work is reaching out and connecting with someone who's already doing what you want to do (or some version of it). Remember, there's no reason to reinvent the wheel.

1. Make a list.
What are some organizations or people who are already doing the kind of work you're interested in (or something similar)?

> **1.5. Break it down.**
> What do you specifically like about these/them?
> Their cause? Their philosophy? Their business model? Their results? Get clear about what exactly draws you to them.

2. Educate yourself.
Once you've figured out who you want to reach out to and why, do a

little digging. Scour websites to find out more about which organizations they are or, if they're people, which organizations they work for. Don't overload yourself here—there won't be a quiz. This is just an opportunity to learn the basics and make sure you don't waste their time asking them questions you could've have found the answers to ahead of time.

How did they get started?
What issues do they face?
Add one or two more of your own

3. Introduce yourself.
Make a personal connection first. Give genuine compliments. If you know of them or have read about their work, let them know how they inspire you.

"Your talk was amazing. Thank you for all the invaluable work you do."

4. Share your goal with them and tell them why you're reaching out.
Be brief. Be specific. Let them know exactly what you're looking for. Think about the elements of what they're doing that you might like to incorporate into your own heart-work.

Can I call you / meet up with you in person / take you to coffee to ask you a couple of questions / or hire you to help me find out more about _____*?*

Ask for support around a particular question or issue they can help you with. Again, be brief and specific. Let them know why you're there, who you are, and what you hope to gain during your time together.

5. No attachments.

Busy people and businesses often delete long emails, and they won't open attachments if they don't know who you are. So keep your communication clean, clear, and to the point.

6. Do a happy dance!

Seriously. This is big. You reached out. You shared. You owned it like a boss! Celebrate that!

Quick side note: I can't promise you that everyone you reach out to will jump on board or write you back. But I can promise you that more often than not, people who are doing work that they're passionate about, especially work that makes a difference, are happy to help others do the same when they can.

7. They said Yes! Preparing for the meeting.

Get out your handy dandy notebook. Before the meeting, prepare two or three questions (your research from Step 2 will be helpful here). Also, think about how you would reply to the question: *How can I help you?* Get clear on what you'd like to gain from this conversation. Funding. Time. Introductions. Advice. Support. This is your open window.

P.S. Don't forget to send that Thank You note. :)

MESS UP + MAKE MISTAKES

So you met! Great!

Except, sometimes it isn't. Great, that is.

But that's okay, because it's all part of the process.

After all, **when you look back at all the things you've accomplished in your life that you're proud of, I'd be willing to bet that they didn't come easy.** You probably had to work hard. Sometimes really hard. I'd also be willing to bet that you messed up a few times before you got to where you wanted to go, am I right?

And one of the reasons why it finally felt so amazing to succeed was because it wasn't just handed to you. You put in the time. You stuck with it. And Hot Diggity Dog! You earned it.

That reminds me of my first day as a brand new eager substitute teacher and how I got completely worked by a classroom full of devious first graders. Truth. Stop laughing. So not funny. Ok, kinda funny now.

Go ahead. Give yourself permission.

Mess up. Make Mistakes. Fail your way to success.

And the next time you flop.
Don't run away…

Keep on truckin'

KiCK ASS WiTH CONFiDENCE

WATCH MY DUST.

—BABE RUTH

Kick ass with confidence! Y-E-A-H BABY!! I like the sound of that!

We all want to feel sure of who we are and what we're doing with our life, right? That's especially true when it comes to making a difference. And there's nothing I want more for you than to go out and make the world a better place while feeling amazing at the same time.

I've found that once you combine your vision, your heart, and your personal why and then share it openly, genuinely, and confidently, big things start to happen.

But how? Is there a secret? Is there something more I could be doing? What is the answer?

Easy...**Confidence**.

CONFIDENCE:

1. A feeling or belief that you can do something well or succeed at something. 2. A feeling or belief that someone or something is good or has the ability to succeed at something. 3. The feeling of being certain that something will happen or that something is true. (*Webster's Dictionary*)

These definitions make it seem like confidence comes from having it all together. Now as incredible as that might sound, let's cut to the chase.

Confidence is really about **what you believe or think about yourself.** That's it.

Did you notice that every single definition above starts with "a feeling" or "a belief"?

Didn't catch that? Go over it again.

Confidence isn't something you need to obtain or buy or chase. It's actually right here, waiting for you. And you know what's sweet about that? It means that confidence is an option for *everyone*. And you've already got everything you need.

Being confident doesn't mean you're not scared or that you know exactly what you're doing all the time. It just means that you believe in yourself enough to take the next step and put yourself out there.

You ready? GAME ON!
Let's keep going!

KNOW YOUR HEART REASON

Really want to kick ass with confidence? Then this is the number 1 thing you need to know. Something I call your Heart Reason.

You've got to know why the work you're doing or are about to do is important to you. Why do you want it? Why do you want to make it happen?

e.g.: I want to start a nonprofit to help families who've lost a loved one to addiction

Why? *Because I want to work for myself* (Okay, that might be true, but what's the deeper reason?)
Why? *To give back* (Again…true. But what is deeper than that?)
Why? *So other families going through the same thing I did will have resources and support that I never got.* (Bullseye! There it is…the heart reason. Do you feel the emotion there?)

Your turn to answer.
What's your heart reason? Why do you care?

Why #1: Why have you gotten involved or excited about this issue, cause, or organization? Why are you here?

I'm here because…

Now I'm going to ask you the same question, but you're going to *dig deeper* this time.

Why #2: Why are you here? Why is it important to you? Why have you gotten involved or excited about this issue, cause, or organization? What holds your interest or prompts you to learn more about this issue?

I'm here because…

And one last time. In one small phrase or sentence. Short and sweet.

Why #3: Why are you REALLY here? What keeps you going or inspires you to get started?

I'm REALLY here because…

Now peek back up at what you wrote. Does your heart reason give you goosebumps or bring tears to your eyes? Does it light a fire or spark inside? If not, try again. One last time. Make it personal.

Why #4: Why are you here?

I'm here because…

Do you see the difference?
More importantly, do you **feel** the difference?

Our heart reasons are tied to our emotions and feelings. You'll know it's time to cheer when the answer to your reason makes you *feel* something.

This is where you wanna get to because your heart reason is where confidence and courage live. Your heart reason is your main purpose for doing what you do. It's your fuel for the good work you've done or are about to begin.

DO iT YOUR WAY

Don't ever hide or hold back.
Do you. Be yourself.

We want to know who you are and hear what you think.
What's your take? Suggestion? Solution?
We want to know your opinions, thoughts, and ideas. Share them.

And you have to know this.

There's no wrong way to make a difference. There's only your way.

Talk like you. Write like you.
Dress like you. Come as you are.

Show up with your own flavor and zeal. Get excited the way you do!!! (Even if some people think three exclamation points is too many. Or that putting a happy face :) at the end of a business email isn't normal. *Hee. Hee.*) Do it your way. Be yourself.

When you do things in your own unique way, when you're just being you, you'll find it feels so much better because you're not trying to play a part.

And remember what happens when we feel better?

That's right. Our actions follow.

Feel crappy = Hide in the closet and do nothing. NOOOOOO!
Feel good = Kick ass with confidence and take names. BOO-YAH!

I'm not gonna lie and say that it's always going to be a breeze to do things your own way. Quite often it will feel scary or uncomfortable. But I promise that the more you give it a go, the easier it gets. And once you do…

CONFIDENCE darling. This is where the magic's at.

And you know what happens next?
When you do things in your own way?

You'll Stand Out.

Just by being yourself. Pretty snazzy, huh? Because as you know, there's no one else exactly like you and that's what makes us spe-cial-ized. And it's so damn refreshing...ahhh.

ONE SIMPLE TIP FOR BEING YOURSELF: ♥
Think of an area of your life or in your heart-work where you've been itching to try something new, do something in a different way, or make a change because something just feels off. Write it down. Then circle back to it and do it how *you* want to do it. If it's not right, you'll feel it in your gut. Tweak it and try again. Wanna know how to have the most impact and do your best work? Show up as yourself. The rest will follow.

FOLLOW YOUR GUT

I'm a gut girl.
How about you?

Ever heard someone say *follow your gut* or *what does your gut say?* Yep. For sure. You know what I'm talking about.

Gut = Intuition

But did you know that our gut instinct is actually a real thing? True story. In fact, it's sometimes referred to by scientists as our second brain. Pretty cool, right? Our gut is connected to our emotional lim-bic system in the brain, which deals with emotions and memory. So it really is kind of like our gut has feelings. Who knew? (Cue all the science smarties nodding their heads saying *tell us something we don't already know*.)

While you're working toward your goals, you're going to be making lots of decisions along the way. So to make sure you're cruising with confidence, you can always do a double check-in with your gut. Like this.

Start by asking yourself a few questions...

What do I want to do?
What am I pulled toward?
What matters to me the most?

Then ask: **What does my gut say?**
Listen. Act. Decide.

Trust yourself. You know what to do.
And let your goosebumps be your guide.

ONE SIMPLE TIP TO FOLLOW YOUR GUT: ♥
Checking in with your gut works really well once you've got your head on straight (check in with your thinking) and you know your heart reason (your purpose). Then, when it comes down to the wire and you have to make a hairy decision and you aren't sure of what to do next or you're feeling stuck, scared, or confused, all you have to do is do a quick gut check.

SECRET WEAPONS & LUCKY CHARMS

This is one of my favorite tips and it's something I've been doing for most of my life. That's right—I'm talking about my little lucky charms. Sometimes I like to think of them as my secret weapons. (Shhh…don't tell.)

You know how Superheroes have their thing that gives them their special power? My lucky charms are kind of like that, but they aren't something that's given to us or that we're born with. They're something we choose.

THEY'RE PERSONAL.

They're things we can look at, touch, read, wear, or put in our pocket. Like an object, a piece of clothing, a note, some jewelry, a photograph. And anytime we see them, they remind us of how we want to feel or of a time we overcame or did something we want to remember.

Kind of like when my son Tobin was really little and he'd try on a pair of new shoes. He'd slip on those mini Vans and zip around the store with his arms flying behind him saying, "ME GO FAST MOMMY!" He always wanted to get the ones that made him run the fastest.

Now we all know that the shoes didn't really make him run any faster. But he thought they made him faster. So when he put them on, he ran as fast as he could, believing it was the shoes.

Lucky Charms are our version of his shoes.

They're about **the feelings they represent, the thoughts they trigger, and what they mean to us.**

I can't even tell you how much I love my secret weapons & lucky charms. I have them everywhere in my house and along with me on any given day. Most people would never even notice them, though. That's the "secret weapon" part, because we're the only ones who know *what* they are unless we choose to share. So fun, right?!

I could go on and on raving about 'em, but I'm not gonna give all my secrets away. **Instead I'll just share a few examples.**

So here's what I mean…

A chunky silver metal heart: I bought it on the day I envisioned Revolution Super Love and it's been sitting on my nightstand ever since. Every night before I climb into bed, I see it. Sometimes I pick it up, hold it for a second, and do a quick heart check-in. It reminds me to keep moving forward in bringing something to life that I really want to make happen.

A business card: I carry it in my wallet. It comes from one of my heart-work role models, Dame Anita Roddick—human rights activist, environmental campaigner, and founder of The Body Shop. She gave it to me before she unexpectedly passed away. I look at Anita's card all the time, and it always reminds me of her fierce dedication to creating a values-based business ahead of her time, no matter what criticism she received, and her global vision to eradicate poverty. She was bold. Lively. Determined. And so funny. Her business card makes me smile because it reminds me of her. It also reminds me that I have some of that magic in me.

My Superhero items: A Superwoman T-shirt, my Marvel tank, my lightning bolt ring…the list goes on. They all remind me of my own power. When I wear one of these I think thoughts like: I am brave. I am unstoppable. I can tackle anything.

Are you excited to create your own Lucky Charm + Secret Weapon?

Here's how:

1. Start with how you want to feel.

Answer this: As you think about moving toward your difference-making mission, how do you want to feel (daring, free, excited, happy, supported, fired-up, motivated, driven, hopeful, confident, inspired)? Make a list if you want. Then, pick one to start with.

e.g.: I want to feel *courageous*.

2. Now ask yourself what object, thing, or image reminds you of that feeling? Remember, everyone's *thing* is going to be different. Make it personal to you.

When I think of *courage* I think of...
e.g.: The Cowardly Lion from *The Wizard of Oz*

3. Once you've thought of something that excites you or just feels right, go get it. Either buy it or find a picture of it online, print it out, and put it somewhere you can see it, touch it, or feel it anytime you want a reminder of that feeling.

Don't know where to start? I've got you covered. Here's one waiting for you. Rip it out. Post it up or fold it in half and carry it in your wallet...Nothing can stop you now.

4. Now anytime you want a little extra mojo, check out your lucky charms + secret weapons.

They'll help shift your thinking to being more positive and you'll naturally feel better, braver, and more badass.

What's that you say? Oh yeah, I'll get out of your way: Up, Up and Away!

GET YOUR REBEL ON

You know what we love about rebels?

ATTITUDE

Rebels are...**Bold.** Brazen. Determined.
Rebels are willing to do things that most people only think about.

Rebels aren't worried about sticking to the status quo or rocking the boat. If they believe in something strong enough, they'll take a risk or stick out their neck to make it happen or get what they want.

Sometimes it's necessary and okay to...

Rewrite the Rules.
Ask for forgiveness instead of permission.
Do something in an unconventional way.

Since we're talking about rebels for good, let's not even go there with breaking the law or wreaking havoc and causing unnecessary chaos. Bueller? Bueller? Anyone? Catch my drift? Alrighty then. I'm talking about being afraid or not knowing the outcome but doing it anyway.

Perhaps you've heard about the activist and rebel for good, Julia Butterfly Hill. You might know her as the girl who lived in a tree in the Redwoods for 738 days to take a stand against clear-cutting of ecologically significant forests. Or Banksy, an anonymous graffiti artist and political activist who uses stenciled street art to provoke thought and discussion. Or Reggae singer and songwriter Bob Marley, who advocated for social change through his powerful, and awesomely-vibed, music.

All true rebels for a cause.

Since you might just be starting out with your difference-making work, **here's a personal and simpler example of what it might look like to get your Rebel On.**

While I was starting my nonprofit, Re:Mix, I was in the not-so-fun waiting period to see if I was going to get approval for nonprofit status from the government. At the time, they told me it could take up to six-plus months. Ugh. Lets just say, *I did not want to wait*. I wanted to keep moving forward so I could get my program off the ground. And in order to do that, we needed money.

A local $10,000 grant opportunity was available and I desperately needed it, but here's the kicker: The very first requirement for applying was having nonprofit status and being set up as a 501c3. And there I was, still waiting.

Now, I had a choice. I could quit, give up, and talk about how much it sucked that we could have had a shot at this money or I could GET MY REBEL ON.

I decided to pick up the phone and call the man in charge of the foundation awarding the grant money. This is where my heart-reason came into play. Because this wasn't about me—it was about the youth we were going to serve. I was so committed to creating the program and this opportunity for the kids that I had to at least try.

I told him I wanted to apply. I explained my situation. I was honest, passionate, and real. I spoke from the heart. I laid it all out on the table. And I'll never forget what he said. "Gia, how are you ever going to hit a homerun if you don't get up to the bat and swing?"

What the WHAT?!
Did he just say I could go for it?! Why yes, he did! WOO HOO!

Now that didn't mean I had the money in the bank, but it did mean that I had the chance to apply. And let me tell you—I doubled down and went after it. But because I didn't have a clue about how to write a grant proposal or the money to hire someone to do it for me, I had to figure it out for myself and do it in my own way. Another story, for another day. Let's just say the fear freakout hit, big time.

THIS IS BREAKIN' THE RULES. NOT FOLLOWING THE GUIDELINES. DOING IT IN OUR OWN WAY. WITH NO REGRETS.

Because really, what was the worst thing that could happen? He'd say no. So what?! I can handle that. And besides that's exactly where I already was if I didn't try. (And for those of you who are dying to know, yeah, I got the grant.)

NOW. YOU'RE UP.

How can you step up to the plate and swing?
Is it time for you to get your Rebel On?

ONE SIMPLE TIP TO GET YOUR REBEL ON: ♥

Ask the tough questions. Put yourself out there. Be willing to feel vulnerable, take an extra risk, do what's needed to be done to make the world better than we found it. It's time to knock your socks off my friend. Go for it.

Not sure if it's time to call on your inner Rebel just yet? Try out this quick test.

Introducing the **FUCK YEAH** approach.

You Ready?
This one's so easy it's kinda ridiculous.

So let's get this straight first.
You've got your heart reason figured out? *Aye Aye. Check. Done.*
How about Guts? *Yeah, I'm ready. Roger that.*

But, you still feel like something's off or you're kinda wavering...?

That's right! I'm starting to question what I know I really want to do and it's so annoying!

No worries, give this a go.

If there's something you **think** you really want to do or try but you're **just not quite sure yet** if it's the right next move for you, **all you have**

to do is imagine yourself as if you've already done it. You reached out. You hit send. You said yes. You went for it.

Then, **ask yourself** if it feels like a FUCK YEAH!

What's that feel like, you say?

You know, that feeling you get when you're onto something good or it scares the crap out of you but deep down you know it's the next step you *really* want to take. *That.* That's a Fuck Yeah.

The kinda feeling when you want to pump your fist high in the sky and yell at the top of your lungs…FUCK YEAH B-A-B-Y!

That's what I'm talkin' about!
I'm all in! I did it!

That's when you know how you wanna roll.

In fact, Fuck Yeah is the only exclamation that will do. Because, *oh yeah*, *yes*, and *okay* just don't have the same umph, energy, or pizazz for how damn good it's gonna feel to do it.

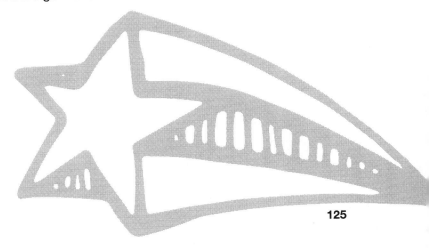

PART
02

WHEN YOU GET STUCK ALONG THE WAY

YOU CAN'T STOP THE WAVES,
BUT YOU CAN LEARN TO SURF.

—JON KABAT-ZINN

 TRUTH + LiES iN HEART-WORK

No one understands. They just don't get it.
Am I really even making a difference?
I'm not doing enough. Fast enough.

Why is this so hard?
I've already tried everything and it doesn't work.

I don't know how.
I'm not smart enough.
If only I was rich.

What if I fail? Screw it up? Do it wrong? Why even try?

GOOD GRIEF CHARLIE BROWN!

Any of these sound familiar? Thought so. We've all got our own version
of smack talk going on in our heads. In fact, some say the average person has around 60,000 thoughts each day, 70% of which are believed
to be negative! No way! Yes-way!

I remember when I really started to examine what was going on inside my head, I felt like I was literally inside my own brain with boxing gloves on beating myself up.

You suck! Left hook to the gut - POW!
You're such a mess! Uppercut to the jaw - POW! POW!
Why don't you have this figured out by now? Right, Left, Right - POW, POW, POW!

I realized I had this whole negative brain dance going on up in there, one I would never win if I kept it up because I was both the defending champion and the rookie in the ring, just taking turns swinging at myself. Either way, I was gonna be down for the count.

Before we take any kind of action to get us where we want to go in one piece, we gotta make sure our head is on straight. And I'm gonna help you by sharing these three truths.

TRUTH #1: YOU DON'T SUCK

And you're not a loser just because your brain said so.
You are not your crappy thoughts.

And get this, just because we think them doesn't mean they're true.
Done. Period. End of story.
NEXT!

TRUTH #2: YOU CAN CHOOSE WHAT TO THINK

Get out! You mean I have a choice? I know, right! I had that same reaction when I first found out.

You bet. We get to choose what we want to think about anything at anytime, no matter what. How wild is that? Just so we're clear, this is so much more than positive thinking and it's not at all about being a Peppy Patty. It's about understanding how our brains work and why we do what we do.

Once you really get this, you can decide to focus on what you want, not what you don't. All you have to do is look at what's happening in your head. Start with becoming aware. **Remember that what's going on up there** (that's right, I'm pointing to your brain) **is what's giving you the results you're getting out here.** That's it.

Don't like you what you see? Then change what you think. Or choose to think something that feels better.

Here, let's give it a go.

Next time you feel off, ask yourself *What am I thinking right now?* Then grab a piece of paper and spill it. Sometimes that's all it takes. Just getting it out of our head reminds us that we are not our thoughts. And we feel lighter.

If that doesn't do it for you, here's another approach. First, check out the thought sentences you wrote down, try them on, and see how they feel to find out which ones are holding you back or don't feel particularly good.

Next, you have a decision to make. You can choose to keep thinking those not-so-helpful thoughts, throw 'em in the fuck it bucket, or flip them or replace them with something you want to think instead. That's right, you can choose to feel better on purpose.

Delete what you don't want. Repeat what you do.

Delete. Repeat.
~~I suck.~~ I'm figuring it out. There is nothing wrong with me.
~~I'm lost.~~ I'm exactly where I'm supposed to be.
~~I'll fail.~~ I'm going for it. I'm on my way. I can do hard things.

So much better, right? Gimme some! Put it up top!

ONE FINAL TRUTH: THE NUMBER ONE THING THAT WILL HOLD YOU BACK OR MOVE YOU FORWARD IS YOURSELF

We don't literally get in our own way, but our stinkin' thinkin' does. All of those crazy, not-so-fun, negative thoughts that keep us up at night and make us start to question anything and everything.

Once we realize that our biggest asset (a.k.a. ourselves) can also be our number one obstacle, then we're good to go. Now when your thoughts get in the way (because we know they're gonna), you'll be ready. And you'll know the steps you need to take to get out of your own way so you can get back to working on what matters to you most.

Remember—**your mind creates your thinking, your thinking creates your feelings, and your feelings drive everything you do.**

If you think you aren't good enough, outgoing enough, tough enough, smart enough, then your actions will follow. And if you think you can get the hang of it, find another way, or give it your best shot, it's as good as done. Want a result you've never had? Then think a thought you've never tried before.

LiES

Now that you've got your head in the game and your heart in the right place, not to mention that boom shakalaka confidence rocking, I'll be darned if I let a few lies get you stuck.

So here they are: **The top three biggest lies you're telling yourself that waste your time.**

Dun Dun Duuuun…

LiE #1: i'M NOT READY

HOLY SMOKE MOLY!

I can't even begin to tell you how many people choose to hang out in "I'm-not-ready-land." Believe me, I've been there myself many a time. It can feel like a nice little safe excuse that we pretend is true.

I am *thinking* about _____.
I'm *about to start* doing _____.
Once I have some downtime then I'll _____.

We say it like it's a fact.
You see, I'm just not ready *yet*.

So here's the truth.

More research is not always better.

Taking more classes and reading just one more book is good for a while.

But at some point *you have to set sail* into the uncomfortable.

Because you're ready enough.

And you know what the biggest benefit is to diving in when you're "not quite ready yet"? You get started. You take the next step. And that action opens the door to what comes next.

I promise whatever you think you need to know or find out more about won't matter as much once you get going. The path from A to Z is rarely straightforward. Almost never does it fall into place perfectly just like our lined-up little plan, no matter how much we might want it to.

And once you get past this pesky lie, you'll find out that you get to spend time doing more of the work you love rather than just thinking about it. Can I get an Amen?!

LiE #2: i'M NOT QUALiFiED

This is one of the biggies that comes up for people as they begin their give-back work. They find things they're interested in doing or are excited about and then they start to second-guess themselves with this doozy of a thought stopper.

"I'm not qualified."

"I don't have the credentials."

Some people somehow convince themselves that they need to go back to school or get XYZ degree in order to help make a difference with an organization or support a specific cause or group.

Being open to learning from others, having the desire to do some good, and showing up heart first is all you need to get started—the next steps will come from there. So whatever you do, promise me you won't keep lying to yourself by thinking you're not qualified. You are needed. Today's the day! Go Get 'em Tiger!

LiE #3: i'M STUCK

No joke—this one might be a favorite go-to lie.

It's so easy to just feel stuck. Stumped. Duped. We tell ourselves that we just don't know what to do or how to keep going. And then we sit there with our frustration, sloppy head games, and we do nothing. Good times.

I think the lie "I'm stuck" shows up for us when we need a reboot. It's our self-check meter and reminder that feeling stuck isn't a bad thing as long as we know it's not true.

If you find yourself feeling this way, try these things out so you can hit stuck where it hurts:

1. Don't think. Just do. Stop where you are, get out of your head, and mix it up. Sprint around the block, ride your dirt bike (or your horse), turn on the tunes, box it out, get out your art supplies, pull some weeds and get your hands dirty.

2. Make a love box for yourself. You may be asking, *Gia, what's a love box?* Funny you ask! A love box is just like it sounds. It's a specific box or drawer that you can fill up with reminders of why you do what you do, things that motivate you, or encouragement from your support crew. For example, mine started with a card. Then a drawing of a heart in rainbow colors that says Mom in the middle that my son gave me when he was little. I threw in a "Free Hug" button I got in NYC, a note from my mom and dad signed with *We Love You*, a thank you card from a friend I helped out, a sticky note from my guy saying, 'JUST BE YOURSELF' written in all caps the way he writes everything. Get the idea? Excellent! Ready to make yours? Have at it!

So next time you're feeling stuck, open that sucker up.
Read, look, touch, see, and know...

How incredible you are.
How much you matter.
And that we believe in you and your big heart.

3. Get out of your own way. Flip back a few pages to the Truth section to find out how.

Still stuck? Ask yourself this one question.

What would Gandhi do?

How about The Dalai Lama?

136

Or Bono, Pink, or Leonardo DiCaprio while we're at it?

Write three ideas here.

LiTTLE ME AND THE BiG LEAP ⚡

When I was about five years old, my mom was driving me to my friend Karen's house in our VW station wagon (sweet ride BTW) to play. I can't quite remember what we were going to do that day, but we were definitely going to have some BIG FUN.

As we got close to her house, I inched my way over to the door (or more like smashed my face against the window), unbuckled myself (remember: no car seats back then), and I was ready to launch. And...I did just that. Which might sound fine and dandy except there was one little problem. The car was still moving.

So, yeah, you guessed it—little Gia went flying out the door and smacked hard on the not-so-smooth, rapidly approaching pavement. And the screams kicked in. WAAAAAA!

I was obviously okay though...I'm still here. Just had some nasty scrapes and bruises and lots of tears. Nothing a little mama love and a warm bath couldn't fix.

But even though I'm sure I was in pain, what I remember most about that day was being so upset about the fact that I had to go back home. Priorities people! DANG IT! My big fun with Karen was gonna have to wait. And I'm sure I gave my mom a heart attack, too (sorry Mom!). Boy, did I mess that one up.

So, I'm sharing this story with you because it's one I think about whenever I get stuck or feel afraid.

I ask myself, *What would make me so excited RIGHT NOW that I would literally jump out of a moving car to go get?* and *What door do I need to push open in order to go get it?*

And I always realize (as cheesy as this is gonna sound) that the only door I ever need to push open and jump through is the one in my mind. You know, the one that can sometimes feel like it's closed up so tightly that it might as well be nailed shut.

As I've learned over and over again, the biggest obstacle in our lives, the one thing that can hold us back most, is ourselves. We've just gotta get out of our own way long enough to channel our inner mini-me's and take the leap. And the great news is that we have 100% control over this obstacle. So no excuses baby.

So now let me ask you…

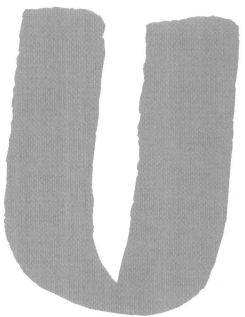

What makes *you* so excited thinking about it that you'd literally jump out of a moving car to go get? (But, um, please don't!) What do you *really* want next in your life? That's the door just waiting to be opened.

Do it with me: 3-2-1-PUSH!

NO MORE WAITING FOR

IT'S TIME

SOMEDAY

YEAH. BUT...

DON'T EVER LET SOMEBODY TELL YOU, YOU CAN'T DO SOMETHING. YOU GOTTA DREAM, YOU GOT TO PROTECT IT. YOU WANT SOMETHING, GO GET IT. PERIOD.

—CHRIS GARDNER, *PURSUIT OF HAPPYNESS*

...THEY SAID

Seriously. Why do we even go there?

This one can totally stop you, and I'm gonna do what I can to make sure that doesn't happen.

Here's the deal.

What other people think? It's about them.
Not you.

Did you get that?
Did you hear me?
Really listen because I'm gonna say it again.

Whatever THEY say, think, or question is what THEY imagine for themselves. It comes from THEIR thoughts, fears, and what ifs.

It really is that simple.

Now don't get me wrong. I'm not saying that you don't want to check in with other people. Or talk with your family, friends, or experts in the field of your hoped-for give-back work. By all means…do that. For sure.

But don't let what they say, think, or feel stop you if you know it's what you really want.

Got it?! You with me?

Because this thing you're going for, the way you want to make a difference in the world and live your life, isn't their desire, purpose, or decision to make. It's yours. And "they" may never understand or really get it, and that's okay.

I've been told many times that I can't make a business around love and helping people who want to help people. "People won't pay for that." "It's not sustainable." "The model doesn't make sense." "Your niche is too broad. Get more specific." The same was true when I wanted to create my retreat for foster youth.

So I'd spin. And spin and spin in my mind. And sometimes I would doubt or question myself and what I was doing. I wasted a few years with this one. No joke. Because I was putting too much weight into what *they* said instead of listening to what I felt and knew I wanted to do.

I finally figured out that in order to get out of my own way and back to doing what I really wanted, I had to be okay with not knowing all the answers. All I needed to know was that I wanted to give it a go. I chose to not let other people's words stop me. Because I didn't believe them.

I listened to my gut and my heart and I kept going. Doing my thing. In my own way.

And I'm so happy I did.

When someone says to me, "You can't do that!" or "You'll never make that work," I say to myself, **Watch Me**.

Fuck you very much.

BUT. i'M SCARED

WOO HOO! Welcome to the club!

I am smiling and jumping up and down saying YES! YES! YES! I'm so happy to hear that!

Not what you expected? HA! That's probably because you think being scared is a bad thing. I'm here to tell you it's not.

Know why?
Because being scared means you care.

And quite often the closer we get to taking action on something we really care about the more the thought "I'm scared" creeps up. And sometimes stage fright does its best to get in the way.

So here's what you can do.

Expect it to show up. Like you're welcoming it to a party. "Hey Scared! So great to see you! I was wondering when you were gonna be here! Thanks for coming and for reminding me that I'm onto something good. Feel free to say 'hi' to some of my other friends, Doubt and Discouraged...

they're hanging out over there in the corner. Then I'm going to politely ask you to not overstay your welcome and skedaddle on outta here." If it still hasn't left yet, simply say...

"Hey Fear...I'd like you to meet my new favorite buddy, The Fear Crusher"

I know. I know. You probably think I've lost it. But humor me and give it a try before you dog on it. I think you'll soon find out that being scared isn't really that big of a deal and that it's just part of the ride. I promise you—if you expect a visit from fear, then it won't surprise you or throw you off your game in the same way anymore. It's just part of the deal. And you'll know why it's showing up for you—to remind you you're onto something.

Not always easy.
In fact just thinking about it makes me wanna puke.
But I've decided I want to give it a shot.

Because the idea of not going after what I want feels worse than being scared.

What about you?

Anything you've been wanting to do or try but for some reason you're not?

Maybe you're scared, too.
It's okay.
We can be scared together.

INTRODUCING: **THE FEAR CRUSHER...** for when the fear freakout strikes

I'd like to introduce you to...THE FEAR CRUSHER!!!
(Spoken in a deep, booming, echoey, raspy voice.)

Don't you just love the name? Can't you just picture it?

I think of a huge, fuzzy monster with a gigantic, slow, blinking eye, standing beside me, who's smiling sly-like just waiting for my fears to pop up, ready to snap open it's ginormous, unhinged jaw to crush every single one of them for me. CHOMP! GULP! LICK!

What does your Fear Crusher look like?

Maybe it's a hot rod with a cape that comes peeling around the corner whenever you whistle or call its name, and then it smashes your fears to pieces.

Or maybe your Fear Crusher looks innocent enough with its ten arms with big bouncy antlers and bright yellow kicks, but then it totally becomes FIERCE and COURAGEOUS once your fears show up, ready to take on each and everyone one of them.

Are you ready call your Fear Crusher to help you out?

While it's super fun to imagine your fears being smashed up to pieces and shown the door, you still might be feeling scared or afraid. If so, let me offer you this.

When you summon your Fear Crusher and it just isn't enough, here are a few things to know and understand.

There are two kinds of fear.
Real and Fake.

Here's the difference.

REAL FEAR is a good thing. It's designed to protect you.

FAKE FEAR can totally stop you if you let it. It's the kind of fear you create for yourself, in your head.

Here's what I mean.

I love monkeys, gorillas, and especially orangutans. I've been drawn to them since I was a little girl. I just never thought I'd be checking one out so up close and personal like the time I came face-to-face with a giant baboon in Zambia, Africa and was saved by a banana. (True story.)

I didn't realize how scared I was until after the run-in. Rightly so. Because I don't think I'd bet on myself if it came down to me versus papa baboon, no matter how many self-defense classes I had taken. After the event happened and a few hours passed, the adrenaline started to leave my body. I felt a little bit better, but I was still jumpy for the next few nights. And I realized that the BEWARE of HIPPOS signs on the lawn? Yeah, they weren't a joke.

This is Real Fear.

Real fear is designed to keep us safe. It turns on our fight or flight instinct. Which is great when we're really in danger and not so great when we're not.

Like when the baboon was gone but my thoughts started to run wild with all of the "what if this had happened?" scenarios and I'd start to feel scared all over again. You see my *thoughts* about the baboon were scaring me, not the actual baboon, as I could easily see he was happily hanging with his family across the river. The fear response I was continuing to have was created by my thinking.

This is Fake Fear.

So I'm gonna go out on a limb here and assume that you're not actually facing your own version of a big ass baboon right now and that there's actually nothing to run from at this moment. Are we good? Okay then. So let's table that kind of fear for now.

And let's address the other kind.

FAKE FEAR

Self-Made Fear.

The kind of fear that can feel so real but it's really all made up in our head. You know what I'm talkin' about.

Self-made fear is just a feeling created by the thoughts we're thinking. It's the kind of fear that feels awful when we believe it has control over us, like it's some kind of wicked villain that's ready to take us down at any moment. YIKES!

But you know what? Now that you know the difference, it ain't got nothin' on you.

You can handle it. I promise.

BUT, WHAT iF?

Welcome to the "What if" mind-funk trick. The one that triggers some serious "dream–stopper" thoughts as one of my favorite authors, SARK, would say.

What if...

I change my mind?
I mess up?
I don't know what to do next?
No one cares?
I cry?

Here are a few quick replies...

So what.

Congrats.

You'll figure it out.

That's a lie.

Let it flow. It shows you care.

There's always a flipside to the "What if" thought stopper.

There's no one way to achieving your mission or purpose to make a difference and it isn't meant to be flawless or perfectly executed. Besides— perfect is boring. Know that bumps are gonna come up along the way. Expect them. That's normal. You're normal. Nothing is wrong with you.

And remember that you have the freedom to change your route or delete as you go. Nothing has to be permanent. And don't be afraid to let your heart bleed every once in a while.

WHAT iF NOTHiNG STOPPED YOU?

BEWARE: A FEW WARNINGS + PITFALLS TO AVOID

THERE IS NO 'THEM' AND 'US'. THERE IS ONLY US.

—FATHER GREG BOYLE // AKA : G-DOG

FEAR OF BURNOUT

Do you ever find yourself thinking there are just way too many people to help and you can't do things fast enough? Or do you feel like your must-do list for your heart-work just keeps getting longer, day after day, with no end in sight? Or do you ever feel like if you don't step in to fix a situation or solve the problem right then and there, no one else will?

How does all of this make you feel?

Are you starting to feel drained, uninspired, or like you're barely hanging on by a thread? If so, take notice, my friend.

Cuz you're headin' straight down the path to burnout city.
And it's time to make a U-turn.

If you find yourself here, know you're not alone and that you can fix it. Burnout is common among people with big hearts and incredible intentions, as we're particularly good at taking care of others and not always so great at doing the same for ourselves.

So what exactly is burnout?

In a nutshell, burnout is what happens when you haven't done a great job of getting the help you need or taking care of yourself along the way.

Once you realize this, there's nothing to be afraid of. You can turn things around or, better yet, be proactive by taking steps to avoid it.

Just to be clear, we're not talking about taking a momentary timeout for a bubble bath or massage and then, *Ta Da! Burnout be gone!* While those are great self-care tips, they'd only be a temporary fix for the underlying issue of *why* your burnout is happening in the first place. Capisce?

To avoid burnout with heart-work, one of the first steps is to understand the difference between helping and rescuing.

HELPiNG VS RESCUiNG

Ask yourself: What role am I playing or have I taken on?
Am I acting as the helper or as the rescuer?

(Hint. Hint.) If you find yourself thinking you have to be someone's savior, my hunch is you're operating in rescue mode. If you ignore your burnout wake-up call and stay here too long, you might find yourself waist-deep in rescue syndrome.

Rescue syndrome is when you believe that the only way for something or someone to change for the better is if you make it happen for them. I promise you that this is a one-way road to burnout.

While you might feel kinda like a Superhero at first when you're off saving the world (which is awesome BTW), remember that for long-term, effective results without burning out, we've got to show up in *helper mode,* not as rescuers.

Still not sure yet?
Check out these two definitions:

To Help: (n) the action of helping someone to do something; assistance. (v) make it easier for (someone) to do something by offering one's services or resources.

e.g. teach, advocate, empower, speak up, lend a hand: teachers, mentors, coaches, tutors, chaplains, counselor, therapist, social worker, etc.

To Rescue: (v) save (someone) from a dangerous or distressing situation. (n) an act of saving or being saved from danger or distress.

e.g. disaster aid relief workers, rescue workers, ER doctors and nurses, firefighters, police officers, armed services, etc.

See the difference?
Here's what I've learned.

Step one to avoiding burnout is to recognize when you're stepping into the role of the rescuer. Then for step two, all you've got to do is flip your mindset.

Rescue mindset → Helping mindset

Instead of…

Enabling → I can assist

Preaching → I can advocate

Lecturing → I can listen

Telling → I can ask questions

Doing it for them → I can pitch in or refer out or empower

It might not seem like much of a change at first. But eventually that heavy feeling you've been carrying and the big weight that's been building will lift off your shoulders. You'll find that you have more energy, your passion will come back, and you will be able to make an even bigger impact. And that's what Revolution Super Love is all about.

CHECK YOUR BLIND SPOT

It's not always the easiest thing to wrap our super loving brains around the idea that someone might not welcome, want, or actually need our help.

We know you care. We see you.
And don't ever change that.

I'm just here to remind you to Check your Blind Spot.

Don't ASS-ume.
Ever.
That we know what someone else needs.

Instead...
Ask them.

How can I help?

Is there anything I can do to support you at this time?

Then really listen to what they have to say.

As we move forward with our heart-work, we have to take a second to make sure our offer to help is welcomed and our intention is in check. *Am I doing this for me or for them?* And we have to do our best to imagine what it might be like to stand in other people's shoes and then go from there.

Here, let's try it out for a sec:

Think about the people you want to help (foster children, abuse survivors, war veterans, people in recovery, etc). Okay. Now, imagine what it might be like to step into their life…

To live where they live. To do their job or not have a job. To have their struggles or pain. To go through what they're experiencing. Imagine yourself in the midst of all the day-to-day stuff. The things we can forget to consider or even think about. Then picture someone asking you how they could help you. What might you say? How would you like to be approached? What might it feel like?

Often, when we choose to see one another through a different lens, we begin to see ourselves as more alike than different. We find out that what we think we know about other people is only a small part of who they really are. And when we take a minute to stand in their shoes, we create a better understanding of where they might be coming from.

No one is exempt from having hard things happen. We all need a hand sometimes. And it doesn't matter what our story or background is—no one ever wants to feel less than or like a charity case.

Be thoughtful. Be respectful. And remember that not all people who need help, want help.

iF YOU REALLY KNEW ME... ⚡

Here's what I'm talking about. Ever heard of Challenge Day? If not, you've gotta check it out (and if you ever have the opportunity to volunteer or host one in your hometown, I highly recommend it).

Challenge Day is an empowerment program that walks high school students through group exercises aimed at self-reflecting, seeing other students with more compassion, and feeling more genuinely connected with one another.

The Challenge Day I participated in was held at the local high school in Truckee, CA. And there's one powerful exercise that the event is known for that has stayed with me ever since. It's called, "If you really knew me."

For this exercise, everyone was divided into small groups, each with six-to-eight kids and a few adult volunteers from the community. All ages (grades 9-12), backgrounds, and social groups were represented. Each small group sat in a circle, facing one another, and took turns going around finishing this sentence:

iF YOU REALLY KNEW ME...

That's it.

One person finishes the sentence at a time. The rest of the group can only acknowledge silently and through body language, like a smile of support or a nod of the head for understanding.

We all took turns. One at a time.
Sharing. Whatever we wanted to say.

Here's a little glimpse of how it might go...

If you really knew me...
You'd know my favorite color is green. (Starts safe)

If you really knew me...
You'd know that I have six siblings and I'm the middle child. (Again, safe)
You'd know that I love chocolate chip mint ice cream. (A few head nods of agreement)
You'd know that I'm afraid of clowns. (Some giggles)

Then it starts to go deeper...

If you really knew me...you'd know that I'm the quarterback but hate playing football. I do it for my dad. (Some eyes look down)

If you really knew me you'd know my brother is dying of cancer. And I feel helpless.
If you really knew me you'd know I'm scared to get below a B on a test. I just can't fail.
If you really knew me you'd know that sometimes we don't have enough food to eat at home.

If you really knew me...you'd know I was bullied and considered ending my life. (A few tears fall, a few heads nod)

As you might imagine, after a while the whole gym was silent except for whoever's turn it was to talk.

Hearts were open. Vulnerability was in the room. A few hugs were shared. Compassion was felt. And in those moments, even if just for a short time, we all connected.

By the time Challenge Day was over, we had learned more about each other in one day than some people find out about another person in a lifetime.

This is what it looks like to really listen and see one another. When we do this, we form a connection and better understanding of each other. We find out that we're more alike than we are different. *This* is what it means to take a moment to stand in someone's shoes.

COMPASSION EXHAUSTION

I can't tell you how many times I've said to my guy that sometimes I wish I didn't feel so much, that I wish I could just turn off my empathy and "be normal" for a little while. But I can't. And honestly, once I get my mind back in check, I would never want to because it's what makes me me.

I'm guessing many of you here are compassion- and empathy-driven like me and that you know exactly what I'm talking about. We understand each other in ways not everyone will get. We want everyone to feel okay inside. To feel whole, happy, hopeful. We don't want anyone to suffer or feel pain. We'd love to fix it all with a magic wand, but know that we can't.

And it becomes a problem when we think that no matter what we do, it's never enough.

Pay attention.
This is your wake-up call to know that compassion exhaustion is about to kick in.

Compassion exhaustion: When your deep sympathy for another who is struggling and your desire to do something to alleviate it takes over and you start to feel run down.

We start to question and wonder, am I even making a difference? Am I really even helping? Am I the only one who cares?

Notice.
Be aware.

Then don't take it on.

Instead, keep taking care of yourself as you go. Ask for help. Get support. Learn how to release and let go. And give people more credit that they're able to step up.

Remember, you're not alone here. You're not the only one who cares. We're all here working on this together.

iT'S ALL ABOUT THE TLC

DON'T BE AFRAID TO SIT IN THE FRONT ROW OF YOUR LIFE.

—UNKNOWN

When it comes to well-being, self-love and self-kindness are not optional for difference-makers...they're a MUST. Okay super-skipper, speed-reader, big-hearted know it alls? Don't whizz past this.

You have to take care of yourself before you can help anyone else.

And if you don't, you might find yourself turning into one hot mess! You know, like frantically eating all the snacks in the house in a matter of minutes (what chips?), spontaneously crying to your neighbor when they say "good morning" (who me?), or lying in a big heap on the bathroom floor wondering how the heck you even got there (WTF just happened?).

Burned out. Stressed out.
It does a body BAD.

Sometimes it happens when you're trying to keep up with everything but you just can't do it all. You get run down, wiped out, and start to feel sick. Ugh. So not fun.

Here's the deal.

Even though it would be really awesome to do it all, you are not the Energizer Bunny. You can't just keep going and going and going without some sort of self-love stuff happening for a reboot. And let's be honest here—even that bunny needs to recharge its batteries every once in a while, right? So, no shame allowed.

Pay attention to your body's signals—tension, stress, fatigue, edgy-ness, or frenzy. Because how you feel is your body's way of telling you what's going on in your head. And believe it or not, they're here to help you.

Feeling a little run down? In need of some self-love or revitalization? If so, give this a go.

LOVE YOU FIRST

In order to help others, you have to love yourself first.

Simple.
True.
Yet, not always easy to do.

Are you being kind to yourself?
Are you taking care of yourself?
Are you listening?

Take notice.

And I'm here to tell you to **quit being so hard on yourself.**

One night I was lying in bed next to my guy.
And I let out a big sigh.

"What's wrong?" he asked.

And I began to list off about five reasons why I suck.

I'm not getting in shape fast enough. Getting fit feels like an endless battle. Why do I even try?

I haven't made time to write my book. What is wrong with me?

I have so many projects that can't come to life fast enough…sometimes I feel like giving up.

Then he rolled over and looked at me and said,

"Gia, you gotta quit being so hard on yourself."

Wow.

He was so right.

I was.

In fact, I was being really mean and saying things I would never say to anyone else. If I heard my son say them I would give him a hug and remind him to be kind to himself.

Why did I have such crazy-ass standards for myself and not for others? And what was all this crap in my head doing to me?

I can tell you. Making me a frustrated, crying, angry mess.

And you know what? **It was all my own doing.**

So that meant one thing. **I could un-do it.**

Sometimes it's about replacing negative thoughts with better feeling ones, and other times it's just about being aware. And that's all it takes. Like a light switch.

So maybe you need someone to remind you like my guy did for me to...

STOP iT.

Quit being so hard on yourself.

Baby steps, buttercup.

Ask yourself this:

What do you need to make sure you can keep going and feeling good? What fuels you? What makes you energized? Excited? Rested? Ready? Connected? Or just plain old ahhhhh-mazing?

Do you need time in nature? A walk through the trees or by the ocean? Do you need time to exercise or eat healthy, yummy food? Or just some down time to rest?
Do you need time to paint, build, or create something with your hands?

Are you in need of some alone time, family time, or an afternoon with friends who make you laugh? Want to pick up a new book, binge watch your favorite show, or grab a copy of your favorite magazine for inspiration?

What do you like to do that helps you feel refreshed?

Do That.

We have to fuel ourselves up because no one else is gonna do it for us. No need to wait 'til you're on empty. Schedule it in. 10:00 am on Tuesday. Self-care time. Re-fuel time. Me time. And make it happen.

Need something more? Go get it.

Need something less? Ditch it.

Don't like what you see? Change it.

You get to take care of you. You get to love you.

PUSH PAUSE

There have been so many times when I've wished I had a magic pause button to push. Just to savor a moment (wouldn't that be awesome?!) or to catch up (the things I could do!) or just chill (whew! If only I had a break) without missing out on anything or time going by. YES! Please! I gotta-get-me-one-of-those!

This usually comes up for me when I'm in go, go, go mode in my mind and I feel like I can't keep up. Or when life is throwing some curveballs my way and my planned schedule gets thrown off. Can't things just wait until I'm ready for them?!

Ever feel like that?

Ever wish you could just yell, "HEY REF...TIME-OUT!"

We know life goes on with or without us. It's not gonna wait for us no matter how much we want it to. **And since there isn't an actual "Pause" button to push, we have to create one for ourselves.**

So, the first thing we can do is know that it's not just alright but it's necessary to push our own Pause button from time to time without any guilt, fear, or pressure. Then we can trust that after our break-cation, everything will still be there waiting for us. We're not ignoring what we

want or need to do, we're not forgetting or pretending not to care—
we're just taking a momentary breather for ourselves.

One of my favorite ways to push Pause is to take a shower. Ahhh…I
love showers. As a rain lover, creative girl, it's where I refresh, let go,
and check in. Some of my best ideas come to me while in the shower.
Sometimes all I need is a few minutes of the water hitting my face and
other times I need to close the drain, fill the tub, and just be there.

What's your pause?
What do you like to do?
Don't have a pause go-to?

Baby, today's the perfect day to make one.

LET iT OUT

Permission to Release.

Anything and everything that you're holding in…let it out.
Anything you've bottled up, shoved aside, or tabled. Now's the time.

Let it out.

Our feelings and emotions are sneaky little buggers. Even if we're sure
we can keep them all neatly tucked away, they'll eventually find their
way out through you. And if we don't let them out, they can turn into
pain, stress, or even disease. They'll eventually catch up to us. None of
us need or want any of that.

Let it out. L-I-T-E-R-ALLY

Cry.
Yell.
Scream.
Have a tantrum. Whatever you need to do for you.

Remember our feelings are just a vibration in our bodies.
Nothing more. Nothing less.

And no need to be afraid…we're all here doing the same thing.

Give it a go.
I promise you, you'll eventually feel better.

MOVE YOUR BOO'TAY!

A great way to take care of yourself is to get your blood flowin' and all those toxins out.

So get movin'!

Walk, jog, run, wiggle, swim, hit the gym, shoot hoops, skate, surf, dance, hula hoop, bike, go to spin class or a barre workout—whatever sounds fun and gets your booty in gear.

It doesn't matter what it is as long as you SWEAT IT OUT!

Taking a break from the screen, getting away from the "office," or heading out of your house shifts the mind and helps us to get inspired and refocused. Breaking a sweat is the perfect remedy to refresh, release, and get back in the groove.

Wish you had some extra energy right now? In need of a pick-me-up? How about a boost?!

Grab your music.
Turn on the tunes and feel the beat.

How about a little Justin Timberlake, G-N-R, Katy Perry, Bruno Mars, or Beastie Boys pulsing through your veins?

3.2.1. Hit it!

Move your Boo'tay!
Because, it works.

And remember—you can go at your own pace. Fast and furious or slow and steady. It doesn't matter.

I can already hear you sayin' "I'm so glad I did that!" when you're done.

PiCK YOUR POSSE

Your Posse. Your Crew. Your Squad. Your Rat Pack.
The people you surround yourself with.

I don't know about you, but positive, kind, supportive people fuel me.

Not only do you want to hang with people you love and who love you back like family and friends—you also want to surround yourself with people you're inspired by and who support you, your heart-work, and your goals. While some of these people might be one and the same, quite often they're not. Sometimes they're the ones we meet along the way. The people we connect with who have similar passions or values as us that make our dream feel more full and alive.

Find your YES people—your personal sounding board that will support you along your heart-work adventures.

Right now. Take a look at your crew. No no, a *deeper* look. Are they fun or inspiring go-getters or are they chronic complainers who always choose to focus on the negative?

Ask yourself:
Who picks me up, makes me laugh, listens to me, and supports me?
Who challenges me in a good way?

When you spend time together, do you leave feeling energized, happy, or just dang good? If not, maybe it's time to find some new people to add to the mix.

That's right.
You get to *choose* who you hang out with.
So why not spend your time around people who add something positive to your life? Right?!

Remember when you were a little kid and you'd just run around saying "hi" to anyone who would listen or who looked fun? Do a little of that. And then a little bit more.

Reach out.

Introduce yourself. Say hello first.

Share your heart and time with people who make you laugh and smile. The people who make your days better. The ones who know what to say (or when to say nothing at all).

Surround yourself with Happy. Ditch the duds.

CELEBRATE ALONG THE WAY

While you're off changing the world, it's super important to acknowledge and celebrate all the little wins you have along the way. I know it can be kinda awkward at first, especially if we're not used to cheering ourselves on, but I promise it gets easier the more you do it and it will make the ride so much more rewarding.

Can I get a...Hip Hip HOO-RAY!?

When we're slowly inching toward our goals, it's so easy to wonder if we've even made a dent. Well, hang on mate (said with my best Aussie accent)! If I were to make a guess, I'd say you've been rockin' it all along, but you gotta take a second to show it to yourself.

Let's play.

Close your eyes (or at the very least, squint).

And take a moment to think about all the things you've been doing over the past few days, weeks, or couple of months.

What steps have you taken towards your goals? What progress have you made so far? What have you crossed off that difference-making To Do list? And let's not forget to include all that life stuff you've been up to, like throwing a fun graduation party for your friend or all that time you put into making sure your Uncle was doing alright after falling and breaking his hip.

Make a list. I'll wait.
Tick Tock. Tick Tock.

Done? Dope.

I'm gonna go out on a limb here and say that I bet you've been kinda busy with some good stuff. Am I right? Can you guess what step comes next? That's right, it's time to say to yourself, "Check ME out! I'm CRUSHIN' it! Look at what I just did!"

Because acknowledging all of our wins is important. It's the part of self-care and self-love that in my opinion we don't get enough of.

And as much as we might want someone to come a knockin' on our door to give us a high-five for rocking out the healthy family meals, throwin' a kick-ass block party BBQ, working our butts off to create that workshop, volunteering to help raise money at the radio call-a-thon, or making it to the gym four days this week, they're probably not going to show up out of the blue. Which is all the more reason to do it for ourselves.

Why?
Because it feels good.
And...

Your body will thank you.

Your mind will celebrate with you.

And it will help you to see your progress along the way. And no matter how silly you might feel doing The Humpty Dance in your driveway, I bet your lips will have no choice but to curl up into a smile.

WOO HOO!
We're all here making some noise for you!

MiNi-PARTY FOR ONE: PERMiSSiON SLiP

Super stoked because you just did something terrific? Feel like cele-brating but you're all by yourself? This is your permission slip (in case you need one) to acknowledge and celebrate you and all the goodness you've been up to. That's right. This is your prescription from Dr. Super Love to shout out a few YAY ME'S and throw yourself a mini-party for one, confetti and all! Yipppeeee!

For: _____(fill in your name)_____
Signed: Dr. Super Love

Never
Underestimate
the Power of a

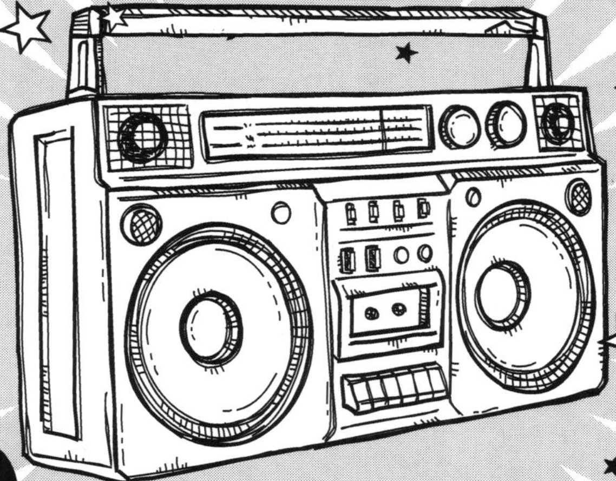

Dance
Break

WHEN LifE HAPPENS

WHEN LIFE THROWS YOU A RAINY DAY, PLAY IN THE PUDDLES
—WINNIE THE POOH

You're busy.

With work. You know, that other job that's paying the bills while you work on creating your heart-work gig.

With kids. We're talking carpools, b-day parties, sports practice, story time, poopy diapers. You have so much on your plate and you have no idea how it's all gonna get done.

With life. Your Grandma needs you. Your boyfriend needs you. Your dentist called to remind you that your annual teeth cleaning appointment (the one that's scheduled six months out) is today, like fifteen minutes ago. You're late.

And GOOD GOSH ALMIGHTY! You just dropped a whole jar of live crickets that were supposed to be lunch for your kid's bearded dragon on his bedroom floor and now you're convinced it's eyeballing you and smirking at you through the glass tank shaking his head....*Seriously, you can't even* feed *me without messing up?! What is wrong with you?*

WHEN LiFE HAPPENS.

Or when that light at the end of the tunnel feels like it's starting to shine brighter and you just know you're *almost* there so you can FINALLY sit down, focus, and work on making the world a better place and…

You get jury duty.

Your power goes out.

Your dad calls and says he needs you to clean out all of your childhood memories that are stored in his house in the next few weeks because he spontaneously started a remodel. Oh, did I mention he lives six-hundred miles away? Hypothetically speaking that is (wink,wink). Hi, Dad!

ARE YOU KIDDING ME UNIVERSE (screamed at the top of your lungs, looking up at the sky)? Please tell me how I'm supposed get my heart-work done when it feels like life stuff just keeps coming at me!

Here's the kicker.

Life is supposed to be messy and un-perfect. Things aren't always supposed to go as planned. And sometimes getting worked over is what it's all about. I know, not what you want to hear right now, but that's how we learn and grow, right?

The goal is to know it's gonna come at ya from time to time. And to not let it hold you down for too long.

Because, isn't it also true that when we finally get past something we once thought was impossible or difficult or hard, or we figure out another way, or we decide to make a different choice or to find the humor in it, we prove to ourselves that we've got this. We can handle this. We can get past this. Sometimes we even look back and say, "Hot dayum, I did that!"

But come on already! When is enough, enough?
Can someone please just make it stop!
I hear you. Believe me, I do.

Here are a few survival tools to make things a little less rough...

#1 LAUGH. FiND THE FUNNY.

If I had to make a guess right now, I'd say that just reading this tip right now might make you want to flip me the bird. Well, just humor me for a moment (pun intended). Ok, you're not there yet. Baby steps. Sorry, I forgot.

Try this one.
Laugh. Find the funny.
Or at the very least, crack a smile.

Need a little help?
Google this: Baby elephant taking a bath.
You're welcome.

#2 ONE MOMENT AT A TiME.

Just do now.
This moment.

Be fully here.
Present.

Yeah, *that*.

But how?

Unplug.
Turn it off
Shut it all down

Your mind. Your phone. Your life.

Take a deep breath.
Ground yourself.
Release. S…i…g…h…

There you are.

#3 KNOW iT. BELiEVE iT. REPEAT iT. YOU'VE GOT THiS.

There are going to be times in your life when you might feel like you need someone to tell you that everything is going to be okay. But they can't or don't or won't, so *you* have to instead.

So here you go. A few of my favorite mantras.

Write them down. Carry them in your wallet or back pocket. Post them somewhere for you to see. For whenever you need them. For when you need something to believe. Or hang on to. Or remind yourself.

That everything is going to be okay.
You are going to be okay.
There's nothing you can't handle.

Know it. Believe it. Repeat it.

Here they are:

I am stronger than I think.
I'll figure it out.
I can handle this.
I am going to be okay.

I've got this.

AND WHEN THE BiG THiNGS HAPPEN

The heavy stuff. Hard stuff. Scary stuff. The things we can't control. The events or situations in the world that can literally feel like they come out of nowhere and take us out.

Things happening on a global level. Like terrorism. Mass shootings. Political unrest.

Things happening in our own hometown. Hurricanes. Floods. Natural disasters.

Things happening that are personal. We lose our job. Someone we love gets sick or dies. Something traumatic happens.

We're talking about the B-I-G things with a capital B.

As huge-hearted people, sometimes life's big things slam us a bit harder. Cuz we care... A LOT. We want everything to be okay. And often we take on more then we should. (Sound familiar?) We focus on helping others and forget to get the help that we need.

That **STOPS** now.

The next time a horrible news story hits, find out what you need to know, then choose to turn it off and walk away. And promise yourself that you won't keep going back for more information, because it's not effective and it definitely doesn't feel good.

Instead, let me offer you this.

Shift your focus away from what happened and toward what you can do.

If you feel an immediate need to help but you aren't sure what to do, dive deeper into what's really needed. The heart-work. Not sure where to start? Flip to pg. 54 All the steps are there waiting for you.

Remember—the big stuff isn't yours alone to handle. We can do it together.

But what about when the really hard stuff hits home? The experiences that are often hard for anyone to understand because they aren't you?

No one else went through what you did, saw what you saw, felt what you felt.

WHEN iT'S PERSONAL. iT'S JUST THAT. iT'S ALL ABOUT YOU.

There is no quick fix or way to rush through hard times, grief, or trauma. Give yourself permission to feel what you feel. Rest if you need to. Listen to your body and what it's telling you.

Sometimes you might not even know what you need, but you know you don't want to go through this alone. Surround yourself and reach out to people you love and trust so they can help guide you and get you the right kind of support.

Then when you're ready, remember that you get to decide what you make this mean in your life moving forward. I believe all of our experiences, even the hard and sometimes unthinkable ones, remind us of what matters most. They show us what we can handle and force us to grow and step deeper into what we're capable of, no matter how difficult.

Remember—asking for help is a sign of strength.
It's you taking care of you and whatever you need to heal during that time.

Inhale. Exhale.

Cool. Next chapter.

PART
03

IMPACT + WHY WE MUST KEEP GOING

{HUGS}

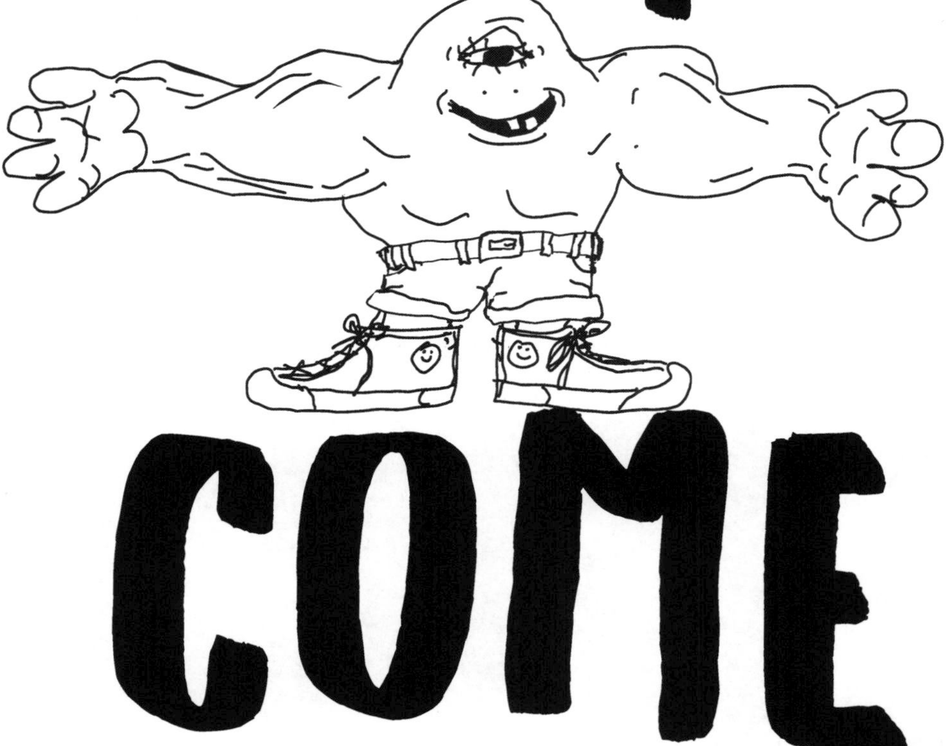

COME ON IN

**TO THE WORLD YOU MAY BE ONE PERSON,
BUT TO ONE PERSON YOU MAY BE THE WORLD.**

—DR.SEUSS

So here's the truth.

We may *never know* the real impact that we're creating...but we don't stop.

We have to believe that what we're doing and how we're choosing to be in the world IS making a difference. And we keep showing up and putting our hearts to work.

One step at a time.

You've gotta know why you do what you do and let that drive you. Remember your heart reason and go back to that anytime you need a little reminder. And seek out other people doing amazing, kind work in the world so you can keep reminding each other.

Another one of my all time favorite go-to ways to keep myself going is to think of the Underdogs. We can't help but love' em. And when we watch or hear stories about them, we find ourselves cheering them on. They give us goosebumps. They inspire us. And they remind us of what we're capable of. So let me introduce to you what I call: The Underdog Difference.

THE UNDERDOG DIFFERENCE

Rocky. Eddie the Eagle. Misty Copeland. Jackie Robinson. *Slumdog Millionaire. Hoosiers. Billy Elliot. Desmond Doss. Seabiscuit. Erin Brockovich. Rudy. The Karate Kid.* Mary Jackson. Katherine Johnson. Dorothy Vaughan.

The unexpected Olympic athlete. The team who should have never won. The undefeated loser rising to the top. The list goes on and I know you probably have your favorites, too. Seriously, I L-O-V-E underdogs. I'm a WAZZU grad for crying out loud— we get the underdog thing on a whole new level. Right COUGS?! G-O C-O-U-G-S!

Here's why we love 'em.
Because underdogs are examples of determination in action.

They're proof of the impossible. The unimaginable.
They deliver the unexpected.

THE UNDERDOG ATTITUDE.

It's all about the thoughts running in their head. The stories they tell themselves. What they choose to believe.

It's all about Grit. Feistiness. Determination.

We won't quit.
We won't give up.
We won't walk away with our head down in shame.

No matter what other people say.

We crash and burn over and over.
We get back up.
We fight.
We keep going. We don't stop.

All excuses off the table.

Cuz...
What we're fighting for...
Going after...
Really want...

Deeply matters to us.

Underdogs remind us that our dream is larger than any fear or setback.

So the next time we get beat, slammed, rocked, or knocked out, we remind ourselves of what we believe. What we stand for. What we're working so hard for.

And we let it drive us. Guide us. Inspire us.
To keep going.
Until we get there.
No matter what.

There's an underdog inside all of us... just waiting to come out.

How bad do you want it?

What if nothing stopped you?

Promise yourself that next time you fall, you'll get back up and go get it.

13 YEARS LATER ⚡

Back when I lived in Truckee, CA, I was a volunteer for the Humane Society. As a family, we fostered and adopted dogs and I was on the board of directors for a few years.

At the time, we didn't have much of a shelter. We shared a small, older, dark building with another city department to house our animals. It was better than nothing, but not great. As a nonprofit, we had a lot of heart, a clear vision, serious dedication, and an amazing animal-loving town supporting us. But we were maxed-out on space. It was past time to build something new.

So we created a projected budget, drew up plans, looked for land, and formed a connection with the animal services department. Then it was time to raise the funds. Word of mouth. Adoption day advocacy. Small events. Local PR. We kept moving toward our big goal. One baby step at a time.

My personal mantra: One day we *will* have an amazing shelter. This will all be worth it. We must keep going. Remember, this was before the crowdfunding days, so things took even more time.

Okay, yeah, yeah. So, what's the point Gia?

Hang with me, it's coming...

Many years later, after my family and I had moved to San Francisco, a friend called and told me that the new shelter was finally finished. I couldn't believe it had actually come to life! I had to see it with my own eyes. So, over the next Thanksgiving holiday while we were in Truckee, we drove straight there.

I have to admit, as we approached the building, it took me a breath or two to realize that it was real. Here I was almost thirteen years after I'd started volunteering for the Humane Society and I was about to walk into the brand new gorgeous shelter. It felt like I was walking into a piece of my heart.

Yes, it happened. This was real.
And I was a small part of it.

A woman greeted us as we walked in and asked if we'd like a tour.
Heck yeah! That's why we were there!

We started by sayin' hey to the cats.

Some peeked at us as from their perches and others zipped down the ladders of their "kitty condos" to share some purrs and get some pets. We snuggled. We watched. We played. Their little meows and greetings were so cute. Something about spending time with them in their new cozy space felt incredible. There was no shortage of love here.

Then we were off to see the dogs. My favorite.
I heart rescue mutts. And if I had a lotta land, I'd have a million of them. Just sayin'.

I'd recently caught sight of a big guy named Ralphie via the shelter's Facebook page and felt drawn to him the first time I saw his cute face.

OMG, my heart skipped a beat. *I hope he's here,* I thought.

I started to get excited and a little nervous as we opened the hallway door. I had butterflies in my stomach. Was Ralphie here or was he in a foster home? I wonder what his personality is like? Uh-Oh…what if I want to take him home? And how am I going to convince my husband? :)

And what-do-ya know.
Guess who was looking up at us from his bed as we passed the first door to our left?

"Ralphie!" I said.

The girl giving us the tour kinda looked at me funny, like, *How do you know him?* She had no idea that I'd been cyber stalking him for months and had a not-so-secret crush on this guy.

Can we go in?
I have to meet him.

She opened the door and he immediately stood up and started wagging his tail while I talked to him. My heart melted. I did my best not to cry. Ralphie wiggled around as he held a ball in his mouth making fun talking noises to us. He rubbed up against our legs and leaned in while he did the please-pet-me swoop walk by.

Time stopped.
I heard nothing our guide was saying.
I froze in this moment.

It hit me.

190

THIS is what patience leads to.
THIS is what fighting for something you believe in feels like.
THIS is what happens when big-hearted people work together.
THIS is what leaving a legacy can look like.
THIS is why we must keep going.

This is why we must continue to share more love and kindness and advocate for what we believe in.

Now here's why I'm telling you this story...

Because as much as I love creating a lifestyle full of heart-work and helping others to do the same, sometimes it sucks. And it's not easy.

Why?
Because quite often it takes time to see the impact.

Which takes patience.
Ah yeah, *that* dirty word.

I'm not a waiter-a-rounder kinda girl. Especially if I'm trying to help someone else or, in this case, help animals find loving homes. I just can't seem to do it fast enough. I'm guessing you might feel the same. But as much as we might want to stomp our feet and clench our fists like the blueberry girl from *Willy Wonka and the Chocolate Factory*, we can't make things go any faster.

And honestly, we don't always get to know how we helped or the exact difference we made. We just have to believe that we did. And keep doing what we love in our own way.

In my experience, every once in awhile, something happens and we get to see firsthand how our time, energy, love, and hard work have paid off.

193

PART
04

THE
DIFFERENCE
MAKER
DOGMA

**BE SOMEBODY THAT MAKES EVERYBODY
FEEL LIKE A SOMEBODY.**

— KID PRESIDENT

WHOO HOO! You did it!

Here you are at the end of the book! You've got ideas brewing, a mini-plan sketched, and some super drive going because you've decided to do what you can to make a positive difference in the world in your own way. You've got the tools. You've been prepped. You ARE ready.

This is it. A booty call for the life you've been waiting for.
You want to live love NOW, and you're gonna leave "someday" to the other guys.

A final send off. Here it is. Your **CREED**

HEART FiRST

Always walk in the room heart first with that spark in your eye…

Make an entrance.
Show up with energy, vision, drive, hope, gratitude, and appreciation.
Leave an impression.

We're talking Raw. Honest. Real.
And so fuckin' passionate that the people around you will want to stop and listen.

You have to believe in what you're doing more than anyone else, even if just for a moment, to take the next step.

Give 'em everything you've got. Like the quarterback in a big game throwing a HAIL MARY and layin' it all out there. Go Big or Go Home.

Show up Heart First.
Every single time.

BE BRAVE ENOUGH TO ACT

We know you're not the kind of person to mess around when it comes to making the world a better place because you were here. We've got enough *watchers* out there and you're not one of them.

You know that in order to make a positive impact in the world, you've gotta take action.

You have to DO something.

Hear something that's not okay? Speak up.
See someone who needs help? Lend a hand.
Notice something that's not right? Take a stand.

Do something about it.
Be Brave enough to Act.

GRAB THE MIC

Got something to say? Say it.

Take the stage.
Pick a side.
Use your voice.

This is your chance to tell the world what you believe, why you care, and how we can rally with you.

Know that while some people will listen, some will help, and a few will pump their fists right along with you, many others won't. It's alright. Just don't let that stop you.

Carpe Diem.
Grab that mic.

Your voice is needed.
We're listening.

LEAD WITH LOVE

You're a leader.

And while all leaders lead, *we lead with love*.

That's the Revolution Super Love way.

We have some amazing role models to learn from…

Think: Nelson Mandela, MLK Jr, Cesar Chavez, and Rosa Parks
Think: Malala Yousafzai, Princess Diana, and John Lennon

Every one of these leaders had a choice. They could have led with violence, anger, or hatred or chose to preach fear, and many would have understood their reasons why.

But they didn't.
Instead, they chose to lead with love.

So do your thing. Make your mark. Do the same.
No matter what. Choose to be a positive role model.
Make it your legacy.

KEEP GOING

By now, as difference makers, we understand this one thing: Our work is never done. We decide to commit. To carry on. To keep truckin'.

You're smart. You know that making a difference isn't always going to be easy. You're going to run into pushback and obstacles along the way. And there might be circumstances that make you angry, frustrated, or frankly pissed off. With heart-work, we know it's just part of the deal.

But here's the difference...we don't stop.

So whatever dreams/goals you're working on, whatever moves your heart, and whatever you're doing to add some more love in the world?

It matters.
Keep going.
It all adds up.

BELIEVE IN SOMEONE

If I could give you only one tip, one call to action, you know, something to do to make an even bigger positive impact in the world and in your own life starting right now, here's what I'd say:

Share these four words. **I believe in you.**

Go ahead.
Tell someone. Right now.
Let them know.

Here's why.
Because they change lives.

In fact, I think they're four of the most powerful words we can hear.

We all need someone to believe in our ideas, our hearts, and who we are without having to change a thing. Sometimes, we just need to know that someone believes in us when we find it hard to believe in ourselves.

So before I go, you have to know that...
I believe in you.

I believe in who you are, what you stand for, and what matters to you most, unconditionally.

Know that you are not alone.
And that we need you, just as you are.

MAKE iT MATTER

It's time to start. To dig in. To get dirty.
To walk our talk.

To seize this moment.
To come together more than we ever have.

Side by side.
With one purpose.

To fire up this Revolution.

To make our time, our mission, and our lives matter.
Cuz baby, we've got work to do.

And it begins here.
Right NOW.

You in?
I DARE YOU
~~Strike~~ that.

Let's make it a...**DOUBLE DOG DARE**

GUTS-N-GO! you've got this

WiTH GRATiTUDE //

**I CAN CONQUER THE WORLD WITH ONE HAND,
AS LONG AS YOU'RE HOLDING THE OTHER.**

—UNKNOWN

For me, writing from the heart in my own way mirrors how I like to live my life, as a journey. And let me tell you … this has been *quite a ride*.

I began writing as a way to heal while my mom's memory health was declining before she passed away in April of 2016. My heart hurt and I felt incredibly alone, lost, and sad. I wrote the hard stories first, one at a time, just letting the words exit my mind.

There were so many unexpected blessings, as well as lessons I learned from her and about myself, while slowly watching the mom I knew fade away. She helped me to appreciate the little things, understand what it really means to be present, and figure out for myself what really matters to me in the end.

I eventually began to shift my focus away from the heavy and toward the feel-good stuff. I wrote about what I hope for and believe in. I wrote about what I value and care about. And I wrote down the stories about people that have made a difference in my life.

I kept writing my thoughts, reflections, and heart on the pages in front of me. "Don't think, just write" was my go-to matra. I eventually started to write the book I wished I'd had years ago while trying to figure out my heart-work.

A few years and 350 pages later, without ever showing a word to anyone, I knew it was time to get this baby wrapped up.

iT REALLY DOES TAKE A ViLLAGE TO MAKE iT TO THE FiNiSH LiNE...

Here's a peek at mine.

To **Debbie Reber**, my beautiful friend, colleague, and kick-ass editor—A gigantic thank you for your time, talent, attention to detail, and patience for my grammar and creative spelling (hee hee). And most of all for your continued support and friendship. Super Hugs!

To **Maddie Kroll**, the only person to have read my entire massive draft of chaos—I'm pretty sure that if it wasn't for you, I'd still be writing in circles or be outta my mind. Thank you for your mad skills, passion, and commitment to my book. You're a rockstar!

ALL AROUND HUGS + LOVE + GRATITUDE TO...

To my **Mom and Dad**, for always loving me and believing in me and being an example of what compassion and kindness look like.

To **Gar**, for being the best big brother a girl could ask for.

To **Justin**, my amazing husband, my guy, my rock. I'm a lucky girl. Thank you so much for your never ending encouragement and support of every single one of my dreams, no matter how crazy. And for believing in me and loving me for who I am through it all. Biggest Smooch E-V-E-R!

Tobin, my son—you have my heart. Keep being you, just as you are, and share yourself with the world. Light it up my boy, as I know you will. You are our future. I love you and believe in you.

And for **Blaze**, my Kansas boy (rescue pup), walking buddy, writing partner, and snuggle bug. I knew we were meant to meet.

BiG GROUP HUG TO Dana Adams, April Cline, Renee Johnson, Julie Inalsingh, Nicole and Michelle Friend, Cheryl Kapchan, Amanda Parks, Dani States, Mike and Marlene Parks, Rosanne Busey, Jerry and Sue Campana, Jessica Riesenbeck, Katie Babkina, Kevin Diamond, Jamey Breen, Doug Bertot, Dan and Michelle Bianchi-Green, Mark and Elizabeth Snyder, Elena Toulios, Michael Bride, Angela True, Amana Ayoub, and Christopher White for the check-ins, phone calls, and high fives along the way. So simple. So meaningful. So appreciated. And to Claudia Forehand for kickin' my booty exactly when I needed it. Mwah!

To my remarkable **Seattle-Bremerton-Bozeman-Reno-San Diego-San Francisco and Australian family** and my friends from all around the world (too many to list ... you know who you are) who have cheered me on and supported my many heart-work adventures over the years. Thank you. You are a big part of this.

A few **"back in the day" gratitude shout outs** go to Mark Keim, Cazzie Palacios Brown, Peter Mayfield, Alan Wong, Cindy Hartzell, Bret Stephenson, Shauna Rossington, Carol Garbutt, Toni Zimmer, Bob Friend, Sam Cobbs, Erin Berecky, Jennifer Bossin and Martha Simon, for trusting in my vision and being a part of Re:Mix foster youth retreat.

You helped to make it what it was. And to Georgia Smith for your friendship, guidance, and dedication to the Truckee Tahoe Humane Society and all of the foster animals you continue to love. I'm in awe.

I honestly wouldn't have made it this far without these three fantastic people with the biggest hearts who've helped me take care of myself along the way … **my TLC team from over the years:** my life coach Kat Kehres Knecht, my acupuncturist Joseph Acquah, and my kickboxing teacher and trainer, Sam Natividad. And to Dyana Valentine for the continued love and kindness since my mom passed away … Extra Big Love.

Three cheers to my many **teachers, mentors, coaches colleagues/ friends** that I'm inspired by and continue to learn from: Debbie Reber, Jody Moore, Lindsley Brooks, Michael Trotta, Natalie Currie, Lachlan Cotter, Pedro Báez, Kanesha Baynard, Jesse Gros, Jen Trulson, Sarah Bamford Seidelmann, Lauren Wilson, Jimmy Tomczak, Bernardo Mendez, Martha Jo Atkins, Michael Bloomberg, Fabeku Fatunmise, Pamela Slim, Brooke Castillo, Martha Beck, Susan Hyatt, Michele Woodward, and the whole Wayfinder crew. Big Squeeze.

A HEARTFELT THANK YOU TO...

Angie Chapman, my mom's caregiver in her final years—there are no words. You exemplify love. I'm forever grateful.

To **Jasper**, the gentleman selling newspapers on Polk Street in San Francisco who always greets everyone with a cheerful ditty hello, even when you're working hard to make ends meet—You are kindness in action. Thank you for sharing your warmth and smile. I so appreciate you.

The **soldiers** struggling with PTSD who have reached out to me—I thank you for your service and acknowledge that we as a country need to do more. I wrote pieces of this book while thinking of you. You are not alone. I see you.

To the **incredible kids in the foster care system**—You inspire me with your courage and strength. Keep speaking up and telling your story. Your voice matters. I'm listening. And to my CASA youth RS, I so believe in you.

To all the **rescue animals** who've crossed my path—Thank you for your love, happy tail wags, and trust. I'll never forget you.

And to all the talented **artists** whose music I danced to in-between writing chapters (3-2-1 HIT IT!)—Your words and beats kept me going … thank you!

To all of my **"imaginary friends"** whose faces blanket my office wall— Thank you for your daily inspiration.

To the **creators, cast, and crew** of the TV shows *The Fosters* and *This Is Us*—Thank you for highlighting humanity, bringing important issues into the spotlight, and helping us truly see one another.

A neighborly shout out of thanks to **Loan Ly** and the oh-so-fun **Soapbox Cafe family** who kept me caffeinated and motivated with your daily smiles, silly jokes, and encouragement throughout the writing of this book. It's finally done! WOO HOO! Thank you all so much!

Most of all, to my **super awesome readers**—Thank **YOU** for buying my book and spreading the word, sharing your time with me, and reading the words I've written. Without you, none of this would matter.

And if we haven't met yet, I say it's about time, don't ya think? Hit me up. (gia@giaduke.com)

I can't wait to see what good we do together.

XOXX,

P.S. Believe it or not, this was one of the more difficult parts of my book to write for fear of leaving someone out. In fact, I'm pretty sure I could write an entire book of gratitude filled with all the amazing people who've crossed my path or have supported me in my life along the way. So if your name isn't listed here, know you are appreciated and incredibly loved. Thank you ♥.

ABOUT GiA

Gia Duke is on a mission to brighten the world through creating more love, compassion, and understanding.

A passionate advocate for nonprofit and charity work, Gia has raised awareness and funds, secured grants for and founded a nonprofit for foster youth, and served on the board of the Humane Society. She has raised tens of thousands of dollars and contributed hundreds of hours to causes in her community and across the globe, from cancer and burn survivors to mentorship programs and aid for Africa. In 2006, she was the recipient of the Profits with Principles Giving-Back Award from The Body Shop At Home.

A certified coach through The Life Coach School with Brooke Castillo and a graduate of the Martha Beck Life Coach training program, Gia is serious about helping people take action to make a difference in the world. She works alongside big-hearted women and men who want to get clear on what matters most and generate the guts to go after it. From pinpointing their cause to finding the people and organizations that need them, Gia helps her clients go from big idea to execution (and everything in between), as well as create a solid plan and keep the momentum until they soar across the finish line. She offers coaching, speaking, online programs, in-person workshops, retreats, and live events.

A Puget Sound native, Gia currently lives in the heart of San Francisco. If she's not at home, you might find her on a road trip with her husband, son, and rescue pug/boston aka bug, Blaze in their VW van, Rust-ell. She thinks farm life might be coming up next.

To connect + find out more + join her community visit: www.giaduke. com

WORK WiTH ME

If you're interested in working with me or you'd like to get more free resources, training, and support, here are a few ways to get started.

1. Mini Session // Got a question about your heart-work or difference-making mission? Want a little help? Grab a fifteen-minute mini-jam session on the house. Just head on over to www.giaduke.com to sign up.

2. Collaborate // Do you have a project, podcast, program, or event you think I'd be interested in being a part of? (Or perhaps you want to produce my TV show?! *wink. wink.*) Hit me up by emailing me at hello@giaduke.com and let's see what we can create together.

3. Sign up // Make sure to sign up for THE BEAT, my not-so-newsletter "fun-letter" full of spontaneous inspiration, happiness, love, and the latest happenings delivered straight to your inbox. (Spam = bad. Super Love = good.) You'll also get instant access to all of my free resources and trainings and have first dibs on upcoming classes, workshops, retreats, and live events! Heck yeah! Who doesn't want some of that?!

SPREAD THE LOVE

If you feel inspired and excited by this book, I'd be so grateful if you'd help to spread the love.

Here are a few ideas:

1. Love the book? Shout it from the rooftop! If that's a little too loud for ya, could you just tell your friends about it?! Like this: "Hey Anne! I just read this really awesome book with lots of tips on how to make a difference and I totally thought of you! You've gotta check it out!"

2. Post a helpful review. It's super easy. All you gotta do is head over to Amazon, type in the name of my book, click "write a customer review," click 5 stars (*hee hee*), and let other readers know what you think.

3. Take a pic! Grab that selfie stick, stage a photoshoot in your favorite cafe or with your rescue hedgehog, take a snapshot, tag me, and share it with your friends! YAY!

4. Email me and let me know what you think! Send me a quote, photo, or video testimonial to hello@giaduke.com. I can't wait to hear from you!

Psst. Don't forget to download your complimentary ***Get Your Heart on Workbook for FREE*** with all of the exercises from the book. Just a little thanks from me to you for buying my book and for helping me to spread the love! Enjoy!

LOVE FOR ALL AND ALL FOR LOVE

HECK
to the
Y-E-A-H!

LET'S DO THIS!

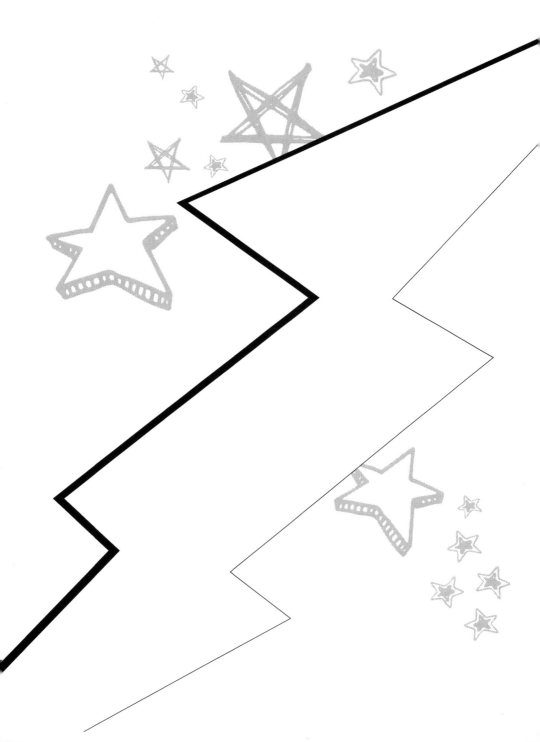

Made in the USA
San Bernardino, CA
26 October 2018